The Relentless Pursuit of Information Technology Excellence

The Relentless Pursuit of Information Technology Excellence

◆

Addressing opportunities and threats in the outsourcing era

ERIC B. TANEFO
Foreword by Dr. Rob Austin, Associate Professor,
Harvard Business School

iUniverse, Inc.
New York   Lincoln   Shanghai

The Relentless Pursuit of Information Technology Excellence
Addressing opportunities and threats in the outsourcing era

iUniverse, Inc.

For information address:
iUniverse, Inc.
2021 Pine Lake Road, Suite 100
Lincoln, NE 68512
www.iuniverse.com

ISBN: 0-595-32935-7 (Pbk)
ISBN: 0-595-66712-0 (Cloth)

Printed in the United States of America

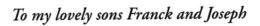
To my lovely sons Franck and Joseph

Contents

Acknowledgments

It is with gratitude that I acknowledge the following persons for their encouragements and contributions. I feel blessed to have a support system with reliable friends and I thank them all for their unconditional support.

To Marie, Franck and Joseph for sharing my pains and joys. We missed a lot of quality time we could have spent together during this project.

To Rob Austin, whose input, time, critiques and guidance regarding the content of the book and the publishing process were precious.

To Roger Johnson, Keith Maynard and Angela Wadley, who took the time to review the various draft copies. Keith and Angela were valuable discussion partners who always found the way to contribute through constructive criticism.

To Maduka Emelife, Bob Muccini and Merrick Olives for their continued support and help with various projects, including this one.

Most importantly, I want to acknowledge two people who inspired me throughout my life. My late father, Samuel Tanefo, taught me the value of hard work. My late uncle, Joseph Tafo, was an inspiring figure who taught me the virtue of excellence.

Finally, I want to thank my mother, Rose Mafopa, for the sacrifices she made for me.

Foreword

In my recent one-to-one interactions with CIOs and other IT managers, the following scenario has become commonplace:

Conversation begins on the subject of a strategic or tactical problem faced by the IT organization. We might be talking about operational processes or digital security or any of today's other "hot" topics. Just a couple of IT enthusiasts bouncing around thoughts and ideas with clinical detachment.

But more and more, after a requisite period of getting comfortable with each other, the conversation morphs until I realize we are talking about troubled relationships. Between the IT function and the rest of the business. Between the CIO and her or his other C-level counterparts. Not so much clinical detachment here. In the most honest and direct manifestation of this discussion, the conversation is about the likelihood that the CIO may be fired in the near future. When discussions reach this level of candidness, they are accompanied by expressions of frustration and fear. These IT managers are perplexed. They don't understand how things reached such a sorry state. And they don't know what to do about it.

In *The Relentless Pursuit of Information Technology Excellence*, Eric Tanefo calls this a "confidence crisis" and he—correctly, I think— quickly zeros in on the issue of trust. Whether right or wrong, fair or not (and I tend to think it's neither right nor fair), IT managers in many organizations have lost the trust previously bestowed upon them by their general management counterparts. To some extent this is simply another facet of the aftermath of the dot com crash. Kicking around IT is cool nowadays. "So you're not all you let me think you were, are you?" is the sentiment inherent in attitudes of today's business press, academia, and business management, toward purveyors of IT solutions in all forms. IT managers can perhaps take some grim solace from the fact that in this regard they probably at least have it better than IT vendors. But when you are worried about whether you'll be fired soon, that solace doesn't go very far.

Into the midst of this difficulty, however, Eric Tanefo arrives with solutions. Working from the advantage afforded him by his considerable industry experience, and with an uncommon understanding of the starting point for rebuilding relationships, he offers concrete and systematic analysis and action. The world has changed rapidly in recent years, and this book takes those changes as its jumping off point. Outsourcing is here to stay. Problems of prioritization and budget allocation remain. Projects are ever more complex and thus harder than ever to manage. And that's just the beginning. What you will find in these pages is not the technical details, but the basic managerial blocking and tackling that a CIO needs to build a new bridge of trust with bosses and business managers. *The Relentless Pursuit of Information Technology Excellence* is nothing less than a call to manage the IT function as a business. IT deserves more respect than it's getting right now, Eric Tanefo suggests, but it also has to transform itself and grow up as a management discipline. It is hard to argue with that logic.

If you are a CIO, an IT director, a front lines IT professional, or a student trying to understand the real problems of managing the IT function—not how to normalize a database design, but rather how to keep the relationships between IT and other areas normalized and operating smoothly—this book can help you. It might even save your job.

Rob Austin
Associate Professor
Harvard Business School

Introduction

The Relentless Pursuit of Information Technology Excellence offers a critical analysis of issues related to the practice of Information Technology (IT) management. Following the debacle of the "dot-coms", there has been a great deal of speculation and doubt about the future of IT. Today, the credibility of IT managers is at risk and we are witnessing a fundamental change in attitude marked by the adoption of aggressive outsourcing measures. Business managers have become skeptical and more demanding of IT executives. They have now set a new mandate for IT managers, which stipulates that they must do more with less. Otherwise, IT services will be continually outsourced.

The past recession has lead to reduced investments, excessive cautiousness and increased interest in outsourcing. Today, we live a period of crisis because IT managers no longer have the total trust of executive management. Meanwhile, some industry experts are claiming that IT no longer matters because it has become a ubiquitous commodity. Such a bold statement does not resonate well with most IT or business practitioners. Nonetheless, it creates an urgent need to elucidate the true causes of the disappointment and frustration with technology.

Undeniably, technology remains a key lever of business innovation and competitiveness. No company can lead unless it uses technology effectively. Nonetheless, practitioners must acknowledge that the IT management process is not subjected to the same level of relentless scrutiny and improvement that seems to be the norm for other business processes. This means that it is opportune to rethink this process, especially in light of outsourcing concerns, to explore all relevant issues and develop durable solutions. *The Relentless Pursuit of Information*

Technology Excellence offers a point-of-view on the issues and formulates specific actions that will address the frustration and challenges of the IT organization. It touches on the rational, emotional and political factors that will define success or failure in managing IT. In addition, it addresses the core issues using an inductive process that emphasizes situational analysis and lessons learned. The result is a clear and realistic roadmap to business value creation.

The book's intent is to trigger a change in attitude and suggest very practical actions. These actions intend to produce long-lasting results as they go beyond any typical suggestion that companies emulate the ones that are perceived to be "best-in-class". One of the objectives is to offer a true exercise of critical thinking and to incite the reader to rethink traditional views and approaches. This book conceptualizes the issues using simple frameworks and tools. It sheds light on probable root causes by drawing on important notes compiled during the last fifteen years. It makes the case that the focus must be on the IT management process and not on technology. It stresses that success requires that business and IT managers espouse a shared vision, continuously improve IT processes, and develop a long-term relationship that withstands turbulent times. The key message is that long-term success hinges on the improvement of risk management practices and the use of IT-oriented intelligence to support the decision-making process. Finally, this book proposes a new methodological framework to guide the development of new strategies that deliver quantifiable business value.

To those who expect a discussion of best practices, I say that the book uses a different approach driven by the quest for durable solutions. It is based on the belief that emulating "best practices" will not produce the type of change that IT organizations need to survive in the new outsourcing era. They must undergo a total transformation and this book is intended to be a compelling transformation blueprint. It uses a set of powerful frameworks to analyze emerging issues, including old concerns that periodically resurface in board and executive discussions. It provides a credible explanation as to why a growing number of people are skeptical about the future of IT. It also suggests creative ways to remedy the situation. The intent is to empower the reader to develop his/her own judgment and explore solutions that outlast any best practices one could offer.

The first chapter provides a historical perspective on the use of IT to improve business process execution and create business value over the last two decades. The chapter specifically discusses the impact of emerging technologies during each phase of the business transformation process and examines the evolution of the business-IT relationship. It summarizes the issues and reveals that old issues do not differ from those companies face today, except that the business-IT relationship has entered a period of crisis.

The second chapter details the root causes of the new confidence crisis that negatively affects the business-IT relationship. It proposes a set of concrete actions that IT managers can take to build a business-IT relationship capable of withstanding turbulent times. These actions address the most common sources of frustration in companies today. They are credible and durable solutions to recurring issues that underpin this critical relationship.

The third chapter discusses one of the proposed actions, which is the transformation of the IT organizations into an internal consulting group. It articulates the merits of the consulting model and suggests that companies embrace it because it is what makes major outsourcing service providers successful. It also suggests the use of think tank structures to improve business-IT collaboration. The chapter discusses the implications in terms of skill development, career development and compensation.

The fourth chapter focuses on IT processes. It specifically highlights improvement opportunities and discusses outsourcing issues and risks. The objective is to identify process changes that could improve effectiveness in a business climate dominated by outsourcing. There is no mention of a particular best practice. Rather, the chapter presents a set of creative solutions to issues that continue to plague IT processes.

The fifth chapter expands on the need for and the value of an internal source of intelligence that can enable smart IT decisions. It makes the case that companies can still improve IT effectiveness if they institutionalize an internal performance measurement process. Furthermore, it details the conditions that will foster an effective use of gathered intelligence.

The sixth chapter focuses on the practice of risk management and highlights the bias towards risk control. It suggests that IT executives change their attitude towards outsourcing, better assess risk and willingly involve outsourcing service providers whenever appropriate. This chapter establishes a new approach that defines the conditions that are conducive to the involvement of external providers, especially in the project delivery area. This approach can be used to devise more effective outsourcing strategies driven by project risk analysis.

The seventh chapter describes the transformation agenda that will help IT organizations create quantifiable business value in the future. It paints the "big picture" by offering a view of important factors that will redefine the role of the IT organization and shape new Business-IT strategies. It lays out a transformation path that organizes all actions discussed in this book into a short- and a long-term action plan. It also elaborates on a strategic blueprint that must guide the development of successful business-IT strategies. More importantly, it explains why technology will continue to be a strategic weapon and a growth engine for many companies in the years to come, therefore making the case that IT will continue to matter.

In my judgment, this book will be a successful endeavor if it enables you to develop new creative ways to address business-IT management issues, irrespective of your level of passion or comfort with technology. It is an important guide for current and future IT professionals. I welcome your comments and suggestions. I can be reached via e-mail at erictanefo@msn.com.

1

When IT executives struggle to remain valued business advisors

1.1 The new confidence crisis

In recent years, skepticism has become the dominant theme of discussions and articles debating the future of IT. Within corporations, there is a tighter control of IT expenditures and a revived interest in return on investment (ROI) measurement. The emerging trend is the intense and sustained focus on cost reduction and increased productivity, symbolized by the "do more with less" mantra. As a result, we are witnessing an unprecedented and relentless push for outsourcing. To say the least, there is a great deal of frustration, speculation and uncertainty regarding the future of IT.

Besides the noticeable skepticism of business managers, the most remarkable event is the recent 180-degree move away from exuberant optimism to frightened pessimism. It is hard to conceive that such a sudden mood swing is the simple result of difficult business conditions. There is an unprecedented level of frustration with IT. *Harvard Business Review* recently presented a controversial article entitled "IT Does Not Matter", which echoes a sense of discontent. In sum, its author partially blames it on the hype surrounding IT and suggests that technology has become an easily accessible commodity that no longer represents a vital source of competitive advantage.

Putting the blame on technology hype is wrong

Although the world knew successful business ventures before the technology era, it is undeniable that IT is a driver of competitiveness today and will remain a key component of any modern business. It would be hard to find a group of individuals who would like to go back to the times when desktop computers or spreadsheet programs did not exist.

Today, the products of technology innovation are more complex and mass-marketed. Technology has become part of our lives and our society has become addicted to it. As individuals, we glorify new all-in-one camera-computer-phone-organizers although they require an increasingly higher level of technology literacy for an effective use of standard features. In the case of companies, IT professionals continue to dream about replacing their various business applications with a single software package capable of supporting all imaginable business processes. Surprisingly, technology is now on the radar of most CEOs and it is now an important topic discussed in such documents as 10Q, 10K and annual reports.

Unfortunately, our addiction to technology has sometimes driven us to make poor purchasing decisions. Recently, IT magazines revealed enormous challenges and disappointments with large-scale software implementations at several major companies. In a few cases, the situation resulted in an important loss of revenue for the company and justified unpleasant lawsuits against IT vendors. As technology overwhelms us, it becomes an easy target of questioning, especially under difficult circumstances.

With the recent acceleration of technology innovation, some practitioners and consultants are concerned that we might reach the highest level of productivity that can reasonably be expected, therefore creating a situation where the quest for additional productivity gain negatively affects the society. Not surprisingly, this debate resurfaces every time a breakthrough in technology makes it possible for companies to rethink the way they operate. One wonders if this legitimate concern reflects a fear of change or the belief that companies must be socially responsible. If we recognize that technology has been the driving force of positive change in our society over the past decades, we must admit that it is wrong to blame it for our failures. In other words, the logical focus of investigation ought to be the IT management process, which is the process companies use to make IT-related decisions.

Putting the blame on the IT management process is not fair

Companies have taken IT seriously over the past years and have devoted a great deal of time, money and energy on improving the decision-making process regarding the acquisition, use, operation and retirement of IT assets. Since the beginning of the eighties, many consulting firms and researchers have studied the subject and offered guidelines, blueprints and methodologies for effective management of IT. In the late seventies, academicians such as Professor Venkatraman (who was lecturing at Boston University) proposed a model for analyzing the many ways companies could ensure the alignment of business and IT priorities. His framework on *Business/IT Strategic Alignment* is a powerful tool that many consulting firms continue to use.

IT effectiveness became an important topic during the nineties with the increased focus on benchmarking and the growing interest in best practices. Later, surveys published in reputable IT magazines continue to mention the same areas of concern. It seems as if experts, who have been studying the issues, have been unable to prescribe durable solutions. Although the serious disappointment with IT management (unsatisfactory project success rate, perception of increased cost for less value) is undeniable, the root causes are more serious than it appears.

IT management does not happen in a vacuum. To be objective, the analysis of the causes must consider the evolution of business priorities as they set the context for IT decisions (i.e. strategic intent, governance). IT issues evolve because business aspirations/goals change over time. The recurrence of similar concerns proves that one subtle aspect undermines the execution of the IT management process. Observations made by practitioners and consultants indicate a growing lack of total trust between business and IT managers.

1.2 Developing an objective analysis of the situation through a review of the recent business transformation process

To develop an objective and analysis of the issue posed by the frustration with IT, it is important to review the business transformation process over the past decades. This review enables us to better understand the role technology has played so far and study the dynamics of the business-IT relationship.

The analysis decomposes the business transformation process using the S-curve (a tool often used by business strategy practitioners to analyze the evolution of an industry) and discusses each transformation stage. The beauty of the S-curve model is that it evokes the emotional cycle and reflects the fact that businesses go through optimistic and pessimistic phases the same way individuals go through ups-and-downs. This important characterization forms the basis of the analysis of the attitude or mood changes in the business-IT relationship. One can picture a business transformation cycle that starts with a period of optimism followed by a phase of excitement eventually ending with a phase of disappointment. In exceptional situations, disappointment leads to depression. Nonetheless, a renewed sense of hope always takes over and triggers the re-emergence of optimism. The S-curve offers a perfect illustration of this undeniable reality.

Every transition phase that separates two consecutive transformation stages is extremely important. It represents a period of chaos or smooth evolution (Figure 1.1) and directly affects the dynamics of the business-IT relationship. The analogy with the emotional cycle is quite enlightening. It reveals important clues that explain the current frustration with IT.

Figure 1.1—The two types of transition

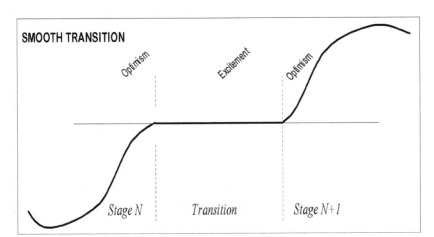

SMOOTH TRANSITION

Optimism
Excitement
Optimism

Stage N | Transition | Stage N+1

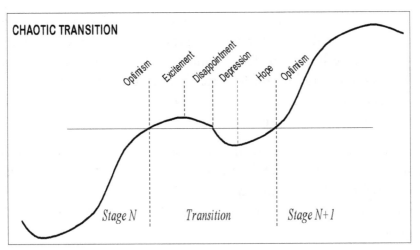

CHAOTIC TRANSITION

Optimism
Excitement
Disappointment
Depression
Hope
Optimism

Stage N | Transition | Stage N+1

The beginning of a transformation stage (S-Curve) often coincides with the introduction of a new technology. There is new sense of *optimism* because companies seek the opportunity to gain a new competitive advantage. IT vendors and the media embark on a promotion campaign to create hype around the new technology. Consultants, who seek to develop and sell new services, endorse the technology and lend a hand to technology marketers. Overwhelmed by aggressive promotion campaigns, the business community ultimately feels the need to test it. As a result, they invest in a pilot and/or deployment project.

As the project nears completion, the business-IT relationship grows stronger. The entire leadership team is committed to its success and is anxious to realize expected benefits. It is a period of *excitement*.

After the project is completed, the team proceeds to identify and quantify delivered benefits. When delivered benefits do not meet expected benefits, tensions arise between business and IT representatives and create a period of *disappointment*. As it often happens, unforeseen production issues emerge. Extra effort and additional resources are required to solve the problems.

When emerging technical difficulties are not resolved quickly, they create a sense of disappointment that negatively affects the credibility of the IT leadership team. The situation eventually leads to *depression*. When the problems are finally resolved, the atmosphere changes for the better and the company is moves on to tackle the next stage of the transformation process. This marks a new period of *hope*.

The subsequent sections offer a detailed analysis of the various transformation stages over the last two decades. They provide invaluable insights, which ultimately reveal the root causes of the growing frustration with IT. Four distinctive stages describe the recent transformation path (Figure 1.2).

Figure 1.2—Business transformation path

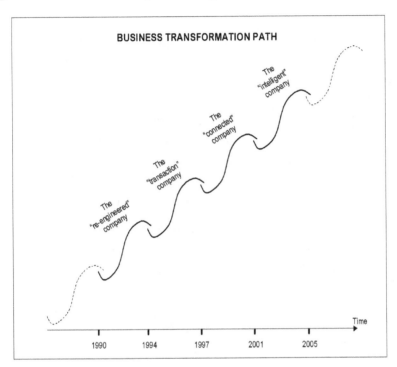

The era of the "re-engineered" company (1990–1994)

The early nineties clearly marked the beginning of the great technology era as personal computers, networking technologies, and relational databases opened up a new world of opportunities. Without hesitation, companies embraced these technologies and took advantage of a computing architecture called client/server, which represented a serious alternative to proprietary mainframe and minicomputer systems sold by IBM, Digital Equipment, Bull and others. Client/server systems enable the distribution of processing power between personal computers and affordable servers. Along with these technologies, sophisticated graphical user interfaces enabled the design of business applications that were more intuitive than the mainframe programs, which used character-based terminal emulators.

Meanwhile, business consultants suggested a new approach to process organization aimed at breaking down old functional silos within enterprises. This new paradigm, dubbed Business Process Re-engineering (BPR), promoted cross-functional processes. It delivered significant cost savings (elimination of redundant tasks and resources) and enabled a renewed focus on the creation of value for customers or the enterprise itself. To support the analysis of processes, researchers and consultants began introducing activity-based costing, which shifted the focus from product cost accounting to process cost measurement.

From a business standpoint, emerging technologies were able to yield significant productivity gains as employees collaborated better to perform value added business activities. The client/server model presented a compelling value proposition and fitted together with BPR. The new technologies facilitated the deployment of decentralized infrastructures that businesses needed to support their geographical expansion. Business managers appreciated the opportunity to redistribute computer resources to improve customer interactions and ultimately provide superior and personalized customer service.

From a technical standpoint, client/server meant that reliable and flexible infrastructures could replace proprietary mainframe computers. The deployment of local area networks translated into major cost savings and the migration to client/server technology enabled the transformation of the IT infrastructure to the benefits of employees and customers. Powerful software products improved human interfaces and contributed to increased productivity (e.g. spreadsheets, word processors, groupware/e-mail, meeting and workflow management tools). It was during those years that companies started adopting Enterprise Resources Planning (ERP) systems such as SAP R/3, which enabled the automation of re-engineered business processes.

In a "re-engineered" company, the case for technology adoption was extremely appealing. On the benefit side, companies drastically improved their internal productivity and tremendously empowered employees to better interact with customer (e.g. access to product data, querying a database for inventory level, access the production planning system to determine the availability date, commitment to a realistic delivery date). On the cost side, companies achieved huge savings as they moved away from proprietary mainframe systems and improved operating efficiency.

The scope of benefits was limited to the company (internal productivity), which made it easy for IT executives to deliver on their promises. The technologies worked mostly, and this fortunate circumstance had a positive impact on the business-IT relationship. IT executives became credible advisors to their business peers and the business-IT relationship improved.

Satisfied with the early results of business process re-engineering projects, companies continued to rethink their processes with enthusiasm. Next, they wanted to gather and analyze business transaction data to devise new strategies to develop profitable relationships with their customers. This next stage was about capitalizing on the investments in client/server technology. This was a logical move that translated into a smooth transition phase.

The era of the "transaction" company (1994–1997)

As companies continued adopting BPR, the consulting community focused on the development of methodologies and tools that would support *rapid business process re-engineering*. ERP solutions continued to emerge and new vendors introduced niche products focusing on customer relationship management (CRM) and supply chain management (SCM). IT executives favored the deployment of wide area networks (WAN) interconnecting local area networks (LAN). At the same time, they deployed more complex and highly distributed computing environments requiring sophisticated middleware solutions.

Expanding IT infrastructures under favorable business conditions (a period of economic growth), companies found themselves processing more business transactions. They seized the opportunity to capture and mine transaction data to gain insight into customer purchasing patterns. The focus was now on knowledge management and data warehousing. They captured large volumes of data into ERP, SCM or CRM solutions and enabled business managers to perform sophisticated statistical analysis using executive information systems (EIS). Managers then used findings to streamline the supply chain and refine marketing strategies (customer segmentation, promotion and channel strategy). The benefits from improved management of supply and demand were adding to internal productivity gains. The new dominant theme became the efficient management of the extended value chain (i.e. supplier-company-distributor network).

From a business standpoint, newly introduced technologies enabled the enterprise to increase its knowledge of customer buying patterns and preferences. Business managers gained a keen understanding of client and channel profitability and continued to decentralize business processes to the benefit of employees and customers. Managers liked the fact that they could structure and analyze transaction data to uncover opportunities to improve sales and service, which enabled them to develop loyal and profitable customers. Ultimately, companies developed rich knowledge bases that empowered employees to make informed decisions. The new paradigm was knowledge-based process re-engineering, which optimized the utilization of resources and production capacity, improved sales and marketing effectiveness, and effectively addressed supply and demand issues.

From a technical standpoint, the adoption of new technologies represented an enhancement and extension of existing technology capabilities. Companies needed to speed-up the processing of a bigger volume of transactions on a global scale. The context was ideal for the type of technologies put forth and vendors successfully advertised the technological prowess of their products.

In a "transaction" company, technological innovations revolved around transaction processing (i.e. robust relational databases, middleware product and analytical tools). As companies continued to redesign their processes, they asked for benchmarking data to assess their relative performance against other players. Consultants fulfilled their needs by offering regular benchmarking reports and best practices. At the same time, ERP solutions evolved to offer sophisticated decision-support tools. Business executives were enthused by the possibility to mine a vast amount of transaction data and better understand the economics of their business. They were finally able to run their company using sophisticated dashboards designed around specific performance indicators.

Technology continued to have a strong appeal as economic times were favorable, which enabled IT executives to easily secure funding for large implementation projects. The scope of benefits grew beyond the company to include customers and suppliers. The business-IT relationship reached its climax.

As business leaders continued to explore the possibilities offered by technology, they sought to extract value from their interactions with suppliers and customers. Around that time, the technology community determined that the Internet could become the backbone of future e-commerce transactions and improve the collaboration between companies, suppliers and customers. This technology, that proved to be a powerful collaboration tool in the scientific community, was adopted by businesses without hesitation. Many businesses rushed to transform themselves into e-businesses and they did it with limited regard for effective due diligence. Quickly, the new dominant theme became the maximization of value derived from external connections. Businesses were now looking to be better "connected" to one another. The transition period would be short and without major disruptions.

The era of the "connected" company (1997–2001)

Towards the end of the nineties, the world experienced the Internet revolution. Companies became excited about the possibility to interact with anybody, anywhere and at any time using a cheaper communication medium. Governments and companies organized major efforts to develop information superhighways that would transform the Internet into a commercial and robust transaction platform. Apart from becoming the backbone of a new distribution channel, the Internet enabled the creation of new business models that would completely modify the relationships and interactions between companies, suppliers, customers, partners and competitors. Moreover, it leveled the playing field for small businesses that had no chance to successfully compete with well-established brands in the past. Any company simply needed a sexy web site and a dot-com address to gain visibility in the market place, regardless of its size or level of capitalization. Old companies worried that a cool web site could have the same or even bigger impact on customers than a traditional marketing campaign leveraging an established brand. Taking advantage of this situation, millions of entrepreneurs started new dot-coms with hopes of redefining the rules of the game to their advantage. It was the era of the connected company.

Consultants advocated new business models dubbed e-marketplaces and classified them as business-to-consumer (B2C) or business-to-business (B2B) platforms. The B2C e-marketplaces improved the shopping experience by enabling electronic auctions, catalog-based e-procurement and community-based information sharing. The B2B e-marketplaces improved the exchange of goods and services between businesses. They also stimulated the creation of purchasing consortiums, thus enabling companies to consolidate their purchases on a global scale and achieve substantial cost savings.

The e-business fever swiftly spread throughout the rest of the world, thus posing an enormous threat to old brick-and-mortar companies that were late or hesitant to alter their business models. Soon, most "dot-coms" would be in financial trouble, having spent enormous amounts of cash on television ads (e.g. Super Bowl ads) and facing a delay in revenue generation caused by the slow adoption of e-commerce. Many promising dot-coms disappeared overnight and others were acquired by brick-and-mortars. Nonetheless, ERP, CRM and SCM solutions still provided important capabilities and vendors made them Internet-compatible.

From a business standpoint, the Internet offered a cost-effective way to reach untapped customers on a global scale. Companies could use a combination of off-line and on-line channels to optimize their marketing, sales and service processes. Furthermore, the Internet lowered the barrier to entry in most markets, making it easier for companies to penetrate new markets.

From a technical standpoint, the Internet drove the development and promotion of robust and scalable processing platforms powered by web and application servers. It also put the Java technology at the forefront of innovation in the areas of software development, middleware solutions and e-business solutions. Companies enthusiastically invested in immature technologies that enabled content management and video streaming. In some cases, they experienced costly project failures. In the end, questionable purchasing decisions undermined IT managers' credibility and made it difficult for them to champion and promote business strategies that called for the implementation of creative business models. Meanwhile, the operational risks inherent to the Year 2000 bug forced companies to think about upgrading their application portfolio. They deployed new e-ERP, e-CRM and e-SCM packages that were Year 2000 compliant.

In a "connected" company, the scope of benefits encompassed the company, its customers, its suppliers and its partners. Although the prospect of new business models initially generated a lot of excitement, it ultimately created a lot of pain and distrust. The few companies that emerged from the adventurous "dot-com" period found themselves confronted with an economic recession. Companies had invested in immature technology products and some of them ended up writing-off these investments. During that same period, some IT vendors went bankrupt and others disappeared in mergers/acquisitions. The NASDAQ, which peaked in March 2000, began to fall and ultimately fueled the growth of IT pessimism.

Furthermore, privacy and security issues hampered the growth of e-commerce. The business community felt betrayed by IT experts and started dismissing new ideas. The nascent skepticism fueled a growing interest in outsourcing. In the meantime, the deteriorating economic situation magnified the financial challenges caused by unwise technology investments. Executives felt the urgency to deploy more sophisticated decision-support solutions and improve their management control capabilities. The new dominant theme was business intelligence and companies painfully moved on to the next stage of their transformation. Under these circumstances, the transition period was quite painful.

The era of the "intelligent" company (2001–2005)

Following the collapse of the dot-coms, surviving companies sought to reassure their shareholders that they could rebound. This became the top priority as a few giant corporations (Enron and MCI Worldcom) shocked the world by filing for bankruptcy protection after their management teams reported misleading financial results. The stunning news reverberated throughout the world and created a great deal of indignation because it meant the end of operation for many suppliers and sub-contractors. Shareholders became anxious and regulatory agencies pressured business managers to consider all possible means to prevent more unsuspected bankruptcies. Business intelligence solutions offered the possibility to improve management and regulatory reporting functions. They would also help managers gain some insights into the company's financial position (financial intelligence), customer profitability (customer intelligence) and supplier performance (supplier intelligence). The mandate for managers was to better allocate the company's assets and drastically reduce costs.

From a business standpoint, the many complaints of investors and shareholders led to the introduction of the Sarbanes-Oxley law, which made Chief Executive Officers (CEOs) and Chief Financial Officers (CFOs) of public companies accountable for the accuracy of mandatory financial reports. This new law established a deadline for compliance, which pressured executives to launch critical risk management and security audit projects. The truthful and timely communication of financial figures was imperative to quickly restore investors' and analysts' confidence. Frustrated by the emerging crisis, business managers initiated direct negotiations with major outsourcing providers, putting their IT managers in an uncomfortable position.

From a technical standpoint, the implementation of business intelligence solutions became a matter of urgency because of the new legal requirements. Nonetheless, these requirements drove additional investments in tools that would enable the integration of all operational systems. The need to improve information management and sharing motivated vendors to promote wireless data access systems. New storage management and security solutions successfully fulfilled some of the needs. On-demand computing became an attractive model, promising that users could access externally managed computing resources the same way any household accesses electric energy.

In an "intelligent" company, the necessity to comply with new regulations and reporting requirements dictated IT investment priorities. The scope of benefits grew to include the investor community. In the end, IT executives found themselves in a difficult situation, having to handle new relationships with outsourcing vendors and struggling to remain trusted business advisors.

Table 1.3 summarizes the key steps and issues that characterized the business-IT transformation process in the recent past. It emphasizes the trends and events that have created the conditions for the frustration echoed by a few analysts.

Table 1.3—Summary of analysis findings

	"Re-engineered" company (1990 - 1994)	"Transaction" company (1994 - 1997)	"Connected" company (1997 - 2001)	"Intelligent" company (2001 - 2005)
Key strategic theme(s)	Adopting a process-based management philosophy to eliminate inefficiencies and redundancies created by functional silos	Mining transaction-related data to better understand the economics of the business, refine marketing strategy and increase revenue/profit	Redefining the rules of the game by implementing innovative business models	Complying with new regulatory requirements and reducing IT costs through outsourcing
Core technologies	Client/server model enablers: - Relational databases - Networking technologies - Personal computers - UNIX-based servers - User productivity solutions	Client/server model enablers: - Wide area networks - Data warehouses - Data mining solutions - ERP, CRM and SCM solutions	• Internet • e-ERP, e-CRM and e-SCM solutions • Web and application servers • Content management solutions	• Business intelligence solutions • Enterprise application integration technology • Storage and digital technologies
IT value proposition	• Redistribution of processing power to support BPR initiatives • Adoption of flexible, non-proprietary and open standards (more choices) • Reduced maintenance fees	• Increased knowledge of customer buying patterns and preferences • Optimization of resource utilization • Sales/marketing effectiveness • Efficient supply chain	• New business models • Cheap and reliable sales/marketing channel • Year 2000 bug fix • Continuous improvement of ERP, CRM and SCM solutions	• Real-time access to insightful information captured in various data warehouses • Accuracy and timeliness of financial reports
Scope of potential benefits	Company	Company, customers and suppliers	Company, customers, suppliers and partners	Company, customers, suppliers, partners and public
Outcome	Nimble and agile companies poised for growth	Business expansion aided by favorable economic conditions	Collapse of the "dot-coms" leading to an economic recession.	Difficult business climate, nervous investors and regulatory agencies
Business-IT relationship during transition	*Good*	*Excellent*	*Weakened*	*In crisis*

1.3 Grasping the trust issue

The analysis of the business transformation process over the past decade reveals important trends and clues that explain the confidence crisis that currently destabilizes the business-IT relationship.

Analyzing the evolution of the business-IT relationship over past decades

The accelerated pace of technology innovation has raised the level of sophistication and driven companies to continuously replace old applications and systems with more complex ones. This has become a vicious cycle. On one hand, vendors continuously focus on increased sophistication to make sure that their products dazzle customers. On the other hand, customers have developed an addiction to technology to the point of valuing the technical features of a product over its true benefits. During the era of the "connected" company (1997–2001), technology innovation reinforced the belief that the Internet could definitely revolutionize the way we do business. Some experts even suggested that technology should shape business strategies and this notion created some tensions among business and IT executives. In hindsight, it seems as if IT-minded people lost sight of the true purpose of technology as they fell in love with it. These events have definitely contributed to the current atmosphere of skepticism.

It is also clear that business and technology leaders all felt excited by technology-enabled opportunities that ultimately became nightmares. As they dreamed about leveraging the Internet to gain access to well-guarded markets, they badly misjudged the complexity of the task, underestimating the many obstacles brick-and-mortars overcame to develop those markets. One could hardly find a more ambitious goal. Ultimately, the lack of realistic expectations resulted in disappointments and created the condition for a confidence crisis. Through the review of the recent business-IT transformation process, it appears that the scope of expected benefits quickly grew beyond the boundaries of the company to include every possible domain (i.e. customer, supplier, partner, public). Although a widening array of benefits meant more opportunities, it rendered the execution of proposed strategies more difficult. As they lacked focus, companies took considerable risks in pursuing very ambitious projects.

It is interesting to note that each phase in the business transformation process was marked by its own set of economic circumstances. Today, we are still recovering from one of the longest recessions and the business environment remains volatile. As result, we are likely to witness a volatile business-IT relationship. Increasingly, some IT executives are relegated to a position where they report to the Chief Financial Officer and this is a clear indication that they have lost the confidence of executive management and other business peers.

Defining trust

Clearly, past events provide important clues as to why the *credibility* of IT executives has eroded. In some cases, CEOs have severed the *intimate* and close relationships they had developed with their IT executives. This decision has gradually made it difficult for IT managers to remain *valued* business advisors. It is creating a serious challenge that they must overcome by *regaining the trust of executive management and building a relationship that withstands turbulent times.*

The analysis of past events also reveals the key dimensions of the issue. These factors are important variables that define the trust formula.

$$Trust = \frac{Intimacy * Credibility}{Risk}$$

The formula conveys the idea that the coziness of a relationship (intimacy) combined with a sense of credibility increase le level of trust. It also expresses the notion that there is always a risk factor at play, which tends to negatively influence the level of trust. The equation defines the levers of trust and suggests a three-dimensional strategy for repairing a broken relationship. Any credible strategy must therefore address elements of risk from an executive management's perspective, create an environment that is conducive to the development of a close relationship and bridge any credibility gap.

To remain or become trusted business advisors, IT executives must consider similar actions to alleviate the mounting frustration that destabilizes the business-IT relationship. The next chapter discusses some of the root causes of the currently crisis and offers specific guide-lines as to how IT executives can address the trust challenge.

2

Resolving the confidence crisis

The trust formula introduced at the end of the previous chapter reveals important factors that relate to three foundational aspects of decision-making. *Intimacy* relates to the emotional dimension, *credibility* relates to the rational dimension and *risk* relates to context (political dimension). This chapter identifies the sources of the growing frustration with IT. The analysis is limited to the most important root causes. The outcome is a set of important recommendations that should lessen the frustration of various stakeholders.

2.1 Revealing the root causes

When IT executives are probed to gain insight into the most frustrating situations they experience, their responses are often emotionally charged and it becomes extremely difficult to discern the true causes of the problem. Nevertheless, informal interviews primarily suggest a lack of trust, which ultimately results in anything but an intimate and relatively risk-free relationship. The root causes highlighted in Figure 2.1 summarize findings from interactions with IT managers and consultants. Surprisingly, they directly relate to the issues of credibility, risk and intimacy, which relate to the issue of trust.

Figure 2.1—Root-cause analysis

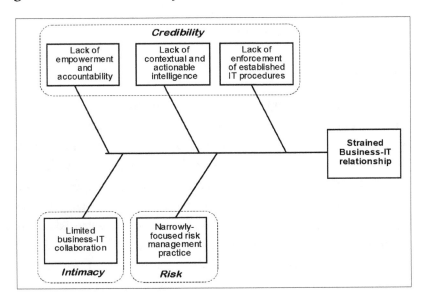

Lack of empowerment and accountability

Whenever any interviewee referred to the notion of empowerment, he/she often alluded to the freedom to take the lead and direct any needed actions. When asked to be more specific, most interviewees mentioned that they were in charge of cost/service centers, which affected their ability to play a more prominent role. Unfortunately, they still confronted the widely spread view that they should primarily focus on keeping the IT infrastructure up and running.

Some referred to their uneasiness with reporting to the CFO. They thought they had earned the right to report to the CEO. They also felt increasingly undervalued and indicated that the limited freedom of action was a considerable factor affecting their credibility.

Because of their limited empowerment, IT executives could not always contribute solutions that address the strategic concerns and aspirations of the business. In this context, they felt that they could not fully play a leadership role and ultimately demonstrate that they deserved to be treated like trusted advisors.

Lack of contextual and actionable intelligence

Another important issue appeared to be the constant struggle and frustration with the budgeting process. Most interviewees dwelled on the difficulty of securing needed funds, even when project proposals supported the aspirations of the business. Some talked about feeling powerless and depressed after they had worked long hours to develop compelling project proposals that were neither approved nor rejected. Unfortunately, IT executives were not always able to give a satisfactory answer when asked what time and resources it would take to deliver a project of a certain size and complexity or what was the typical ROI across projects. It was apparent that they could not back their responses with accurate data or statistics.

In some cases, IT executives did not have the proper tools to develop insights into IT activities. When pressing the interviewees for further information, they would almost systematically refer to the latest report from an external research or advisory group. They simply lacked a source of intelligence that would enable them to convince any business executive that they should be trusted.

It is clear that they needed to build an internal source of intelligence around IT activities to gain the type of contextual and unbiased insight needed to reassure the providers of funds. This would definitely boost their credibility.

Lack of enforcement of established IT procedures

The interviews revealed that most IT organizations had adequate procedures in place. The issue was that they could not always enforce them. Often, a few decisions makers would not follow the procedures. In the end, exceptions would become the rule and people would tend to blame it on the process as if it was not adequate. Often, the power play creates an environment where successful individuals feel that they can circumvent established rules. It also transpired that IT executives did not or could not clearly communicate the consequences of non-compliant actions.

IT executives often lacked the tools to enforce the procedures. They needed to be able to regularly audit the procedures and implement required modifications, when appropriate.

The interviews also revealed that poor compliance negatively affected the morale of the IT staff because it engendered frustrating priority changes and entailed a sudden modification of project assignments, which meant the consumption of precious resources by unscheduled activities. As a result, IT teams would find themselves stressed and put in a situation where they would be likely to fail.

Narrowly-focused risk management practice

During interviews and conversations, few respondents could articulate a proactive risk management philosophy. They all had a reactive approach, which emphasized the audit of operational procedures. They often had difficulty answering concerns regarding the risk profile of their project portfolio.

Generally, they would develop security guidelines addressing data-related, application-related and infrastructure-related risks. They often overlooked the critical analysis of their project success rate. At times, they championed risky projects that did not offer a credible business case and an exit strategy.

It appears that IT executives focused more on operational risk and less on investment risk analysis, an area that is becoming critical because of the outsourcing trend. As a result, they ignored important risk reduction opportunities and this often created the perception that they do not welcome outsourcing. Today, the direct effect is an atmosphere conducive to reinforced skepticism and cautiousness.

Limited business-IT collaboration

When touching on the subject of business-IT collaboration, it was apparent that IT and business representatives did not always speak the same language. There was a need for a communication forum where they could openly debate issues and clear misunderstandings or misperceptions. In some cases, it was interesting to notice that both parties rarely participated in common team-building activities although a great deal of communication happened in technical workgroups addressing technical topics (e.g. centers of excellence).

Surprisingly, few IT workers had an intimate knowledge of the company's business strategy. It was therefore difficult to imagine everybody pulling in the same direction. Certainly, knowledge sharing and improved communication would enable the mobilization of the entire organization towards common goals. One could envision promoting the practice of a very successful company that inscribes its business strategy on the wall in the entry hall at its headquarters. The company made it a goal to constantly remind everyone of and communicate its purpose and aspirations. It was clear that the establishment of new business-IT think tanks or task forces could provide a "safe" environment for business and IT representatives to constructively discuss expectations and concerns.

It is important that business and IT representatives collaborate on various important initiatives (e.g. new product ideas, technology scan, tactical execution, issue resolution) and develop an intimate rapport, which is essential to a healthy relationship.

2.2 Articulating credible and practical actions

To effectively serve the purpose of the business, IT executives must strive to develop a strong business-IT relationship. It is a serious challenge that requires innovative ideas. The goal is to enable a relationship that withstands turbulent times. The trust formula makes it obvious that any credible action plan must consider three axes of intervention.

Enhancing the business-IT relationship through better collaboration

Whatever the internal culture, companies must *consider an operating model that fosters business-IT collaboration by stressing relationship building and development.* With the prospect of relentless outsourcing, IT teams must emulate the type of organization implemented by successful outsourcing service providers. They must foster a close collaboration by replacing technology-focused centers of excellence with a more inclusive think tank structure. Otherwise, they will turn into simple agents responsible for purchasing and auditing IT services on behalf of executive management.

Re-engineering IT processes and developing IT intelligence

Credibility is a prerequisite to regain the trust of executive management. IT executives must consider the following two actions:

- *Re-engineering IT management processes in the context of outsourcing*

  It will be helpful to review and eventually reconsider current practices in light of outsourcing considerations. Understandably, the focus ought to be on strategic and tactical processes, given that operational processes are likely to be outsourced at one point or another. The use of advanced process analysis techniques will help to improve process execution, reduce cost, and ultimately eradicate the frustration with IT.

- *Institutionalize internal performance measurement to develop IT-oriented intelligence*

IT executives can better understand and communicate the value of IT by implementing an internal performance measurement process focusing on IT processes. Hence, they will be able to develop an internal source of IT-focused intelligence, which could improve the decision-making process and give them an advantage over outsourcing service providers.

Deepening the practice of risk management

IT executives must adopt a *proactive approach to risk management by deepening risk analysis and mitigation.* They must consider passing on or sharing risk with outsourcing service providers, and not categorically oppose outsourcing. They must learn from practices in the financial services area and adopt a similar risk management philosophy. This action will result in high project success rate if IT executives use external providers intelligently.

The business-IT relationship is at risk and it is imperative that IT executives listen to frustrated internal customers and take appropriate actions. A change of attitude is essential to regain the support of executive management, especially considering the emphasis on doing more with less. Ultimately, IT executives will recover from this crisis and re-emerge as trusted advisors. The subsequent chapters elaborate on the proposed actions.

3

Implementing a new operating model

Recently, companies have restructured their IT organizations following major outsourcing decisions. In the process, they have reduced their internal IT workforce, overworked the remaining staff and frustrated their loyal employees. Going forward, they must find a way to regain their trust if they want to keep them in the future. They should consider introducing new job incentives, retraining their most valuable players and rethinking the compensation system. One important task in this process is the choice of a viable operating model.

Today, IT executives remain anxious because executive management often reduces the problem to a simple choice between a centralized and a decentralized organization model. They often use the analogy of a pendulum swinging from one end (centralized model) to the other (decentralized model) depending on the internal forces at play in the company. It is critical to examine this issue because the speed of the pendulum dictates the stability or volatility of the business-IT relationship.

The stakes are high and it is important to avoid any simplistic approach, such as the experimentation with different organization models. The challenge is to redefine the role of the IT organization with a long-term perspective. We have known centralized models with shared service organizations. We have also known decentralized models that revolve around autonomous service/profit centers. It is undeniable that over its lifespan, a business will evolve its organization model to successfully address emerging challenges and attractive opportunities. The constant challenge is to make sure that the organization model offers the best environment for the development of required process, people and technology capabilities.

3.1 An assessment of traditional organizational models and views

To develop effective organizations, IT executives must adopt a process-based view that emphasizes the creation and delivery of business value. With the push for outsourcing, IT executives must redefine success, then establish practices that lead to success and finally figure out the best operating model for their organization. It is important to start this analytical exercise because the traditional functional view emphasizes hierarchy and does not reflect a process-focused organization. Today, most IT departments remain organized in functional silos that emphasize task specialization and static roles (see Figure 3.1). This does not fit with a process-oriented structure that relies on teamwork, is multi-disciplinary and conducive to the effective collaboration of business and IT representatives. Without a doubt, old organization models hamper the creation of business value.

IT executives must advocate an operating model suitable to process-based activities. For a long time, IT has supported the re-engineering of non-IT business processes and it is time that the IT management process undergoes re-engineering. As companies continue to embrace outsourcing, success will depend on the sound execution of strategic and tactical activities because operational tasks will be prime outsourcing targets. The IT team must specifically master such activities as strategic planning, audit, program/project management, and relationship management.

Figure 3.1—Traditional IT organization model

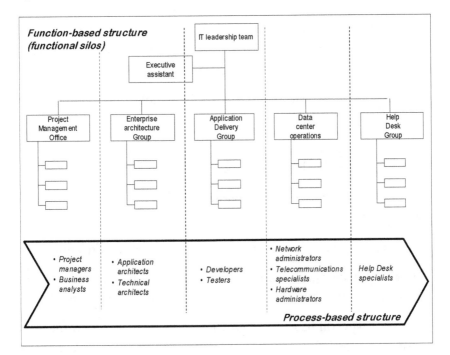

3.2 Rethinking the purpose, focus and role of the IT organization

Because of the new focus on strategic and tactical excellence, the IT organization must redefine its purpose around important processes. It must draw on proven techniques such as business process re-engineering and Six Sigma. The benefits will be considerable because it will lessen the frustration of business executives, who are still wondering why IT executives have difficulties justifying the business value of IT.

IT executives must therefore map all processes and leverage activity-based costing and statistical analysis techniques to improve their effectiveness. In addition, they must track specific performance metrics to identify areas of weakness or strength so that they can help business executives make smart outsourcing decisions. It is a critical task, given that most outsourcing deals amount to billions of dollars over a period of time that often spans more than one technology cycle.

To be successful in the long term, the IT organization must adopt an organization model that fosters flexibility and is driven by the following objectives:

- Deliver measurable business value

- Fuse business and technical knowledge into a reliable source of intelligence

- Effectively manage the portfolio of projects, assets and relationships

- Improve the delivery of critical IT-enabled capabilities and services, even when it involves offshore outsourcing service providers.

IT executives still have the opportunity to regain their rightful place as trusted advisors. To accomplish this goal, they must embrace this new vision.

3.2.1 Shifting from project management to project lifecycle management

Although IT executives have made significant investments to develop their project management capabilities (i.e. methodologies, tools, certification programs), surveys conducted by IT advisory groups continue to indicate a concern with project success rates. Lately, there has been a lot of disappointment caused by the dismal implementation of complex enterprise solutions (i.e. ERP, SCM and CRM solutions). Unfortunately, many IT organizations focus on project execution and tend to overlook other equally important aspects. Particularly, few emphasize the need to master the broader process represented by the entire project lifecycle.

It is important to rethink current training and management practices. In reality, it is urgent to do so, given that project management has become a cross-organizational process involving internal resources and offshore developers. As the quest for better return on investment dominates future strategies, project management will become a more complex process combining three critical activities, namely project design, project execution and project auditing. These activities demand the same level of attention because project design and project auditing are essential to increase project success rate (see Figure 3.2). They provide the type of insight needed to reverse the current situation and restore the credibility of the IT organization.

Using activity-based costing and management, IT executives and their team must develop an accurate cost baseline, which is a critical piece of information for the negotiation of beneficial outsourcing deals. This example reveals the importance of the project design and auditing phases. It clearly highlights the need to re-examine the entire project lifecycle. IT executives must also think about assessing the quality of the project management process so that they can track project success rate, identify predominant success factors and devise a strategy for improving project management. They must be mindful that the IT organization will come under intense pressure as outsourcing service providers attempt to take over important IT processes and services.

Figure 3.2—The focus of project management

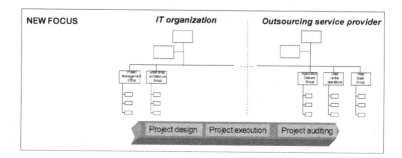

Regardless of the circumstances, the IT team must take the necessary steps to keep the ownership of the company's project portfolio. It is therefore imperative that it excels at designing, executing and auditing projects because such an effort will have a lasting and positive impact on the business-IT relationship.

The following section discusses the challenges inherent to the management of the project lifecycle. It starts with the attribution of a project code and ends with the closure of the project once the different audits are conclusive regarding the recognition of actual benefits. This is an important point because common frameworks tend to consider the closure of a project before the delivery of the last benefit stream, which often occurs well after the completion of the execution phase. The analysis looks at issues and discusses their impact on the business-IT relationship. Furthermore, it offers practical recommendations and analyzes the implications in terms of process efficiency and quality, operating model and governance.

3.2.2 Improving project lifecycle management

The following table summarizes the activities involved in the management of the project lifecycle. Although all activities are important, the initial design phase is even more important because it has a profound impact on project execution and auditing. Perfecting project design can dramatically improve project success rate. For this reason, the analysis stresses project design issues (see Table 3.2).

Table 3.2—project lifecycle management

Activity	Typical tasks	Typical issues
Project design	• Assign project code • Qualify project • Determine key project attributes • Capture/Adjust costs and benefits • Identify project phases • Assign delivery resources • Designate auditors • Assess risk profile and develop exit strategy • Prioritize project	• Meaningless project code • Lack of business sponsorship • Unspecified project categorization • Shallow cost/benefit analysis • Complex project structure • Poor assignment practices • Flawed risk management philosophy • Lack of project-related intelligence • Lack of effective prioritization method
Project execution	• Execute project phases • Control project delivery quality • Resolve technical issues • Conduct review sessions • Produce status reports	• Scope creep • Cost / time overrun • Unpredicted technical challenges
Project auditing	• Assess progress • Assess end user satisfaction • Track and communicate delivered benefits • Close project • Capture lessons learned	• Poor technical quality • Unmet requirements • Poor user acceptance • Benefit shortfall

IT teams will dramatically improve their success rate by addressing the following issues in the project design phase:

• *Meaningless project code*

IT teams sometimes use meaningless codes to identify projects. To facilitate project identification by individuals that are not intimately familiar with projects (i.e. auditors, executives), they should consider a more descriptive codification method and forbid the use of fancy codes. This will save a lot of time and eliminate unnecessary and frustrating investigations, especially when the portfolio consists of several hundred projects.

- *Lack of business sponsorship*

  Often, the project documentation ignores or mistakenly mentions business sponsors. In one case, the project does not enlist the support of any business stakeholder. In the other case, designated business sponsors are not actually involved and there is no way to determine who is blessing the project. Unfortunately, such situations are sources of challenge when requesting funds for projects. The IT team must never consider any initiative that is not endorsed by a business representative.

- *Unspecified project categorization*

  Specific criteria used to define "small" or "big" projects are often poorly defined and unknown to some decision makers. This is an important issue because executive management tends to overlook small projects. As a result, they end up focusing on "big" projects that cost less than the whole set of "small" projects they should be monitoring. Key stakeholders tend to scrutinize a "small" project only if it becomes a "big" or complex one. To resolve this issue, IT executives must work with their business peers to develop a clear categorization method and ensure that size is a meaningful factor in determining the proper level of project scrutiny.

- *Shallow cost/benefit analysis*

  When capturing cost and benefit data, project managers hesitate to involve key business representatives to get a validation of the impact on the P&L statement or balance sheet. The timeline of the benefits rarely takes into account the possibility of future retirement or rollback due to insurmountable technical difficulties. The most illustrative example is the repeal of a dismal ERP implementation, which has unfortunately occurred at many companies. IT organizations must improve cost/benefit analysis by assessing total cost of ownership and considering potential incidental costs (e.g. the cost of an eventual repeal). Otherwise, executive management will continue to question the credibility of project business cases, which will reflect on the credibility of the IT team.

- *Complex project structure*

    A typical project plan depicts a set of activities connected through a web of dependencies and is not necessarily suited for business executives who are more interested in business milestones and benefit streams. Going forward, the IT team should highlight technical as well as business milestones. It will make a difference in "selling" projects to executive management. Decision makers will feel more comfortable when they are given the option to fund a project in several steps subject to the successful accomplishment of specific business milestones (just-in-time funding approach). Additionally, complex project structures make it difficult to address issues related to business sponsorship, funding and project portfolio management. By keeping it simple, companies will also minimize project risk.

- *Poor assignment practices*

    In an atmosphere of uncertainty and cost reduction (doing more with less), the IT employees feel overworked, undervalued and powerless. They rarely object to assignments that do not fit with their skills and aspirations. In the end, they loose their motivation. It is important that IT executives ensure the alignment of aspirations and assignments because poor assignment practices ultimately affect the team's morale and productivity.

- *Flawed risk management philosophy*

  The tendency is to focus on risk control. In some cases, the IT team does not spend the time necessary to properly qualify and quantify project risk. In other cases, they tend to resent outsourcing although it offers the opportunity to transfer unbearable risk to third parties. IT teams must systematically evaluate project risk and explore ways to use outsourcing service providers intelligently. Over time, they will develop effective outsourcing strategies and practices, which will improve their project success rate.

- *Lack of project-related intelligence*

  Knowledge capturing and sharing is not a common practice in most IT organizations. As a result, project managers often lack access to a knowledge base that would provide historical project data, speed-up the development of project charters and summarize important tips to avoid past mistakes. IT organizations must develop a project knowledge base to improve various project design and management activities.

- *Lack of effective prioritization method*

  With the focus on "doing more with less", IT executives should develop an effective prioritization method to ensure that available resources are spent on the most attractive project opportunities. Some are investing in software tools for project portfolio management, hoping to improve the alignment of business and IT priorities and the allocation of financial and human resources. No matter the solution, the prioritization model must consider a multitude of dimensions (e.g. strategic fit, financial profitability, risk) and support a dynamic reconfiguration to enable what-if scenario analysis.

  To become a streamlined and value-focused organization, IT executives must restructure the IT function. To achieve process excellence and improve their project success rate, they must mimic expert practitioners like successful consulting firms. It is imperative that they seriously consider their operating model because it drives many successful outsourcing providers.

3.2.3 Turning a cost/service center into an internal consulting group

Recently, executive management personally initiated the negotiation of IT outsourcing deals at major companies, which sent a clear message to their IT executives. In the future, IT teams must focus on strategic and tactical activities and support the use of outsourcing services providers for the delivery of operational services. To meet this new challenge and remain trusted business advisors, it is important that they exhibit the following distinctive characteristics of successful consulting organizations:

- *Team spirit*

  The most important characteristic of a successful consulting organization is the dedication to customer satisfaction and the idea that the team comes before each individual team member. This is a fundamental notion, which characterizes successful consulting firms no matter how bright each individual consultant is. It marks a difference with traditional IT organizations where technical gurus often dictate the course of action and do not necessarily use other colleagues' input to offer the best workable solutions or recommendations.

- *Strong business and technology acumen*

  Consulting organizations are expected to understand the market space and the technology challenges facing their clients. By the way, no company would hire them unless they know the industry it plays in. As a result, consulting companies have developed rich knowledge bases that house valuable industry information and data. They enrich these knowledge bases by institutionalizing knowledge capture activities.

- *Flexible and adaptive organization*

  Consulting firms are role-based organizations. Consultants are generally flexible, work on diverse issues, learn to use a variety of problem solving techniques and avoid the "one solution fits all" syndrome. This has the effect of stimulating individual creativity and flexibility. Unlike traditional IT organizations, successful consulting firms are not inclined to replicating solutions, and they pay attention to the peculiarities of each situation.

- *Excellence in relationship building/management*

  Long-term success in the consulting world is defined by the ability develop distinctive capabilities (service offerings, people) and build lasting and fruitful relationships with clients. Officers in a typical consulting firm are more than experts or technical gurus. Rather, they develop a network of internal and external connections to win and deliver more projects. Eventually, they dedicate some time to community-building activities and contribute as members of the board of charitable institutions.

  To be successful, IT executives must revamp the recruiting and career development practices to ensure that their IT organization reflects the distinctive characteristics of a consulting team.

3.3 Implementing an internal consulting group

IT organizations must embrace the consulting model because it is an effective model for any organization focusing on strategic and tactical issues. IT teams must excel at solving business issues by developing and sharing business-IT intelligence. They must also perfect the management of the project portfolio, build relationships and optimize the quality of project/service delivery. To enable a transformation into an internal consulting group, IT executives must overhaul the recruiting process, the training curriculum and the compensation system. These actions are essential to effectively mobilize the IT staff.

3.3.1 Rethinking career development plans

The recent wave of lay-offs driven by outsourcing has undermined the sense of loyalty. Companies that proudly proclaimed that their employees were their most valuable assets are now shying away from any slogan of that nature and are quietly acting as if these employees have become disposable resources. It is a surprising turn of events that will create a big challenge when the job market fully recovers. Undeniably, employees will continue to doubt the company's intentions in the future. To repair the damage, companies must rethink their recruiting and career development practices to reflect a renewed commitment to long-term development and empowerment. It is in their best interest to sustain the high level of productivity they have had in recent years. It is also important that they empower their work force to avoid bad publicity and prevent the eventual departure of the most valuable players.

IT executives must foster an environment that values every employee, provide development opportunities beyond technical roles, and motivate everyone by offering exciting projects. They certainly have a chance to offer exciting projects because such boring tasks as software maintenance will be outsourced. Furthermore, they must discourage behaviors driven by the following factors:

• *"Body shop" mentality*

The term "body shop" mentality describes any employee management practices that values routine work and does not attempt to develop individuals so that they can deliver highly differentiated services. The motivation is to recruit people and only use them on projects that require the specific expertise they have. This philosophy reflects a short-term commitment on the part of the executive team. A good example of a "body shop" is a provider of staff augmentation services. New recruiting and career development processes must support the idea of parlaying technical skills into more business-oriented roles. This important evolution must guide the design of new training curriculums. In the end, IT executives will comfort employees who may be concerned that they no longer are valued.

- *Obsession with certifications*

Generally, most employees periodically revisit their resumes to add a few more coded words identifying newly introduced technical certifications. It is almost as if the number of certifications was the best indicator of aptitude. Today, the common belief is that a "good" process manager must be Six Sigma certified or a "good" project manager must hold a certification from the Project Management Institute.

Common practices overvalue certifications and traditional recruiting processes tend to underestimate the importance of people skills, creativity and leadership. In fact, it is not rare to come across PMI-certified individuals who lack the people skills to successfully run a project. On the same token, it is not rare to meet non-certified individuals who successfully deliver complex projects because they have good leadership or people skills and can effectively follow any given methodology. This example highlights the issue with traditional views. It makes the case for the adoption of new recruiting and career development approaches that de-emphasize certifications, focus on breadth of skills and value quality of experience.

- *Role confinement*

The "body shop" mentality and the excessive focus on certification result in the development of monotonous and boring roles. In fact, IT organizations remain hierarchical structures that tend to confine each staff member in a specific role for the duration of his/her career. This is contrary to the practices in consulting organizations, which offer a more dynamic environment and a diversity of roles. Consequently, IT employees tend to resist change because they are used to applying the same solutions to the same problems over and over again. To remedy this situation, IT executives must encourage job rotation. Putting employees in a variety of roles, IT executives should enable employees to hone their IT and business skills and learn to better communicate with their business peers. New recruiting and career development plans must promote job rotation so that employees can quickly acquire the skills needed to become or remain trusted business advisors.

IT executives have the opportunity to regain the confidence of employees. They must make the necessary changes to prevent the loss of talent and ultimately guarantee a good return on training investments.

3.3.2 Reskilling the work force

IT executives must continue to invest in their staff if they want to avoid losing the edge they have over outsourcing service providers, especially regarding strategic and tactical activities. If these providers only seek to take over operational services today, there is a good chance that they will go after strategic and tactical services once they will establish their credibility. It is up to IT executives to do everything necessary to prevent this nightmare scenario. It would be a catastrophic failure given the fact that they are best positioned to defend the company's interests. One can simply imagine what it was like to be subjected to the domination of IBM in the seventies and eighties when it dictated decisions, solutions, prices and ultimately made IT executives believe that they could not be wrong by going with "Big Blue".

Two foundational principles must guide the redesign of training curriculums:

- A balanced mix of strategic, business, IT and people skills (see Figure 3.3)

- A revision of career development plans and compensation systems to encourage the adoption of proposed changes.

The proposed skills characterize the human capabilities that are required to transform traditional IT organizations into successful internal consulting groups that are able to execute strategic and tactical activities to perfection. Companies that reinvest in training will reap significant benefits, including:

- Cost avoidance: employee retention will save the cost of future recruiting campaigns

- Knowledge retention: companies will avoid the loss of knowledge to potential competitors as employees graduate from the firm

As companies entertain the idea of a renewed commitment to training, they could hire a few seasoned consultants who could join the IT team and coach less experienced team members. They could implement a train-the-trainer program to ensure that trained individuals continuously transfer the knowledge to future recruits. IT executives could eventually collaborate with academic institutions to provide the desired training (e.g. executive programs).

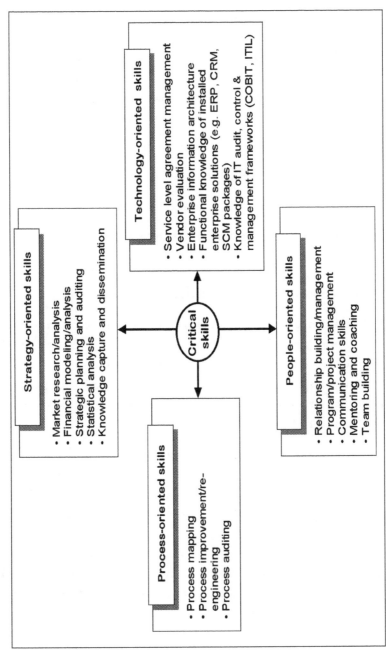

Figure 3.3—Skill map

3.3.3 Upgrading the reward system

It is a very well known fact that what gets rewarded gets done. It is therefore logical that companies revisit and eventually upgrade the compensation system to put in place the type of incentives that will motivate the IT staff to perform as an effective consulting group. In the end, IT executives must reinforce behaviors that enable the following:

- Team spirit (team building and role modeling)

- Flexibility and job rotation

- Quality of deliverables and customer satisfaction

- Relationship building (internal and external relationships)

- Intelligence gathering and sharing

- Positive contribution to group activities (e.g. think tank)

In redesigning the compensation system, companies must think about measurement tools and metrics that enable an objective evaluation of individual performance. The trust that employees will put into the revised compensation system will depend on its objectivity. It is essential that employees believe in a fair assessment of and compensation for their accomplishments.

Finally, any compensation system that is limited to base salary must be reevaluated to include additional incentives such as performance-based bonuses. The reintroduction of stock options is not a silly idea for public companies, given that the new Sarbanes-Oxley law warrants the accurate and timely reporting of financial figures. Nonetheless, IT executives must probe their employees regarding the structure of the compensation plan. It is the least gesture they can do before imposing any scheme based on market surveys and published data that do not take into consideration the internal culture or the specific preferences of employees.

3.4 A word about governance

The issue of governance tends to resurface every time a new technology or economic cycle transform the aspirations of companies. Consequently, governance will remain the topic of recurring debates among practitioners, consultants and researchers.

In the past, upper management owned the issue of governance, which often drove internal politics. Understandably, it frustrated IT executives as they were ignored or could not be an important voice during governance discussions. The difficult part was that they were asked to follow imposed rules even when they undermined their ability to perform their duties effectively.

Today, many experts attempt to promote a more collaborative approach. In fact, two different advisory groups have taken the lead in developing a bank of information and a set of best practices and assessment tools addressing IT governance.

In the United States, the IT Governance Institute has developed a generally accepted standard, focusing on IT security/control and governance. The proposed framework, known as COBIT, offers a set of measurement tools and best practices covering more than thirty IT processes.

In the United Kingdom, the Office of Government Commerce (OGC) has developed an IT infrastructure Library (ITIL), which they claim is the most accepted approach to IT Service Management in the world. ITIL also develops best practices drawn from research in international public and private sectors and offers some interesting implementation and assessment tools.

No matter the internal culture, business and IT executives must collaborate to define governance rules affecting strategic and tactical processes, including outsourcing management. For those critical activities/processes, they can use a simple matrix to define the players (i.e.

all stakeholders), the tasks (process steps and decision points) and the nature of their involvement (role). Such a tool can provide a synthesized view and facilitates the communication/diagnosis of governance rules. In fact, it can easily show the concentration of power or the lack of involvement of a key stakeholder in decision that requires a consensus. Finally, this tool can help to summarize lengthy (and sometimes outdated) guidelines described in operational guides.

4

Re-engineering IT processes in the context of outsourcing

With the sustained interest in outsourcing, IT organizations are virtually in competition with external service providers. Having to do more with less, they are expected to spend their energy on value-added activities and think strategically to help executive management make smart outsourcing decisions. This is important because a decision to reverse or scale back an outsourcing deal will profoundly affect any IT organization.

Outsourcing requires that IT teams analyze the advantages and drawbacks of various sourcing scenarios. Nonetheless, it is important that they continuously improve all processes before they can figure out the ideal conditions to pursue outsourcing opportunities, something more insightful than a spontaneous push for immediate cost reduction. Eventually, they will have to revise their outsourcing strategy and relationships over time to ensure that they are contracting with the best providers. This certainly highlights the need to perfect the analysis of service levels.

Initially, the IT team must consider leveraging standard process improvement techniques (e.g. Six Sigma) to re-engineer internal processes. In doing so, they must precisely identify major cost drivers and compute the cost baseline that decision-makers should use to gauge the attractiveness of outsourcing proposals. Additionally, they should identify process pain points to better understand if and how the IT organization delivers business value. This is the minimum task required to establish the conditions under which outsourcing will yield important benefits in the long term. Furthermore, IT teams must address collaboration issues to maximize the contribution of all parties.

IT executives must reexamine the IT management cycle and start an investigative process to develop durable solutions to existing issues. Otherwise, executive management could force major outsourcing decisions upon them, which will ultimately put their success at risk. This chapter provides an overview of IT processes. It represents an important component of the re-engineering effort that is essential for developing a world class IT organization. It examines internal issues, offers creative solutions and examines the execution challenges posed by outsourcing.

The discussion covers eight sub-processes forming a generic IT management cycle (see Figure 4.1). The structure of the cycle reflects a looped process that drives the use of IT to improve business performance. It also reflects a self-reinforcing mechanism aimed at maximizing business and IT effectiveness.

Figure 4.1—The IT Management Cycle

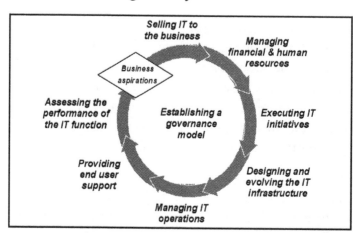

4.1 Process One: Selling IT to the business

4.1.1 Purpose and key activities

This process represents one of the most challenging and frustrating tasks for IT executives. It is a task generally owned by the IT leadership team. The challenge is to successfully develop and promote a strategic plan that is blessed by executive and/or board members. It requires analyzing the business context and the performance of company's operations, identifying newly required IT-enabled capabilities and ultimately restructuring the IT project portfolio (see Figure 4.2). The objective is to get the commitment and support of key stakeholders as well as secure funds for IT initiatives that are critical to the execution of the company's business strategy.

The following activities describe how the IT team identifies, documents and promotes IT project opportunities.

- *Analyzing the business context*

  The process starts with the analysis of business aspirations (business plan), a strategic audit focusing on business performance analysis and the thorough review of opportunities or threats posed by emerging market trends. By examining specific business processes, the team is able to identify the business capabilities that are essential to address performance gaps, seize new opportunities or guard the company against potential threats.

- *Identifying required IT capabilities*

  After uncovering needed business capabilities, the team proceeds to identify technology solutions that the company can leverage to build such capabilities. It then looks for equivalent assets that might already exist to avoid creating redundant solutions. Then, the team designs new project proposals that it submits to the board for approval and funding purposes. During this design phase, the team addresses the issues relating to business risk, technology risk and sourcing. It also develops a cost/benefit analysis of the proposed project(s).

- *Redesigning the project portfolio*

  When new projects are accepted, they become part of the project port-folio. The team then uses a prioritization process to determine the re-allocation of available financial and human resources. Eventually, it decides to freeze or cancel ongoing projects that fall at the bottom of the newly prioritized project list. Such adjustments are also made when business priority changes warrant a review of project priorities and the dedication of available resources to the most viable projects. This char-acterizes what is commonly known as business/IT strategic alignment.

Figure 4.2—Selling IT to the business (process summary)

	Analyze the business context	Identify required IT capabilities	Redesign project portfolio
Input(s)	• Business plan • Balanced scorecard • Research findings (market and technology trends)	• New capability needs • Help desk issues list • User surveys (applications) • Current initiatives • IT capabilities map	• Charters of new initiatives • Current project portfolio
Activities(s)	• Understand forces affecting the competitive environment • Relate business aspirations to business metrics • Assess historical performance trend • Qualify opportunities/threats	• Identify newly required IT capabilities • Review "make" vs. "buy" strategy • Review strategic alliances • Design charters of new initiatives	• Design new programs and projects with detailed business cases • Prioritize consolidated project portfolio • Develop tactical actions (project cancellation, freezing or continuation)
Output(s)	• New business capability needs	• Charters of new initiatives • IT strategic plan	• Updated project encyclopedia

4.1.2 Concerns and proposed actions

Table 4.1 presents a list of concerns and offers action(s) that can improve the effectiveness of the process. These actions range from a re-investment in research activities to the deployment of adequate decision-support tools. Failure to successfully execute this process could result in considerable frustration, especially when the long hours put into the development of project proposals are fruitless. The more credible the IT leadership, the better its chance to expedite the process, gain the support of key stakeholders and secure the funds needed to execute viable projects.

4.1.3 Outsourcing issues and risks

The analysis of the business context often involves external strategy consultants because they think independently and can therefore develop a more objective assessment of the internal situation. Their independence of judgment is valuable because a faulty assessment could result in costly mistakes down the road. Outsourcing this task could make it difficult to mobilize the IT team and develop a consensus around opportunities and threats. The IT team should be part of or own the process. External experts add value when they are used to essentially validate the thought process and the findings.

A risk of bias exist when specifying and suggesting the type of solutions that could provide newly required IT capabilities. Increasingly, consulting organizations are establishing strategic partnerships with third parties (i.e. system integrators, software firms) to address all the possible needs of their clients. They are therefore tempted to recommended the type of solutions that will benefit these partners. To mitigate this risk, companies should emphasize due diligence, including a visit of client sites where the technology is already in use. Outsourcing this part of the process could be counterproductive, given that internal teams often have the best knowledge of existing capabilities. Typically, internal experts do not suggest the use of a new technology unless they are confident that it will work for internal clients. This is important to ensure user acceptance as many technology implementations have not always survived a rejection by internal customers.

Finally, the rationalization of the IT project portfolio is a critical task that the IT team must automate using convenient tools. This activity would be difficult to outsource if the IT team must remain accountable for the prioritization of project activities and the re-allocation of resources.

Table 4.1—Concerns/actions regarding the selling of IT to the business

Concern	Action(s)
Organizations dedicate less time to technology scanning activities and market research, which impedes innovation.	• Establish a think tank to bring together business and IT representatives so that they can collaborate on such activities as idea generation, process innovation, technology scan and project proposal development. • Consider internal activities as a source of new patents and incremental revenue.
IT executives have less influence and fewer opportunities to shape the business strategy.	• Be open-minded, have the company's best interest at heart • Do not oppose outsourcing but proactively seek beneficial relationships
The IT strategic plan remains a separate document, which makes it difficult to perceive the strategic alignment of business and IT priorities.	Combine both plans into a single document to improve the clarity and maintain the coherence of proposed actions.
The business strategy is often unknown to many employees, making it difficult to maximize mind share.	Build a simple performance model using strategic themes, business drivers and metrics to communicate the business strategy without revealing confidential data.
IT executives lack the tools to re-compute project priorities in real time when business priorities are altered.	Implement an algorithm that combines the various dimensions (e.g. risk, financial profitability, strategic fit).
Often, the documents describing the current state of IT capabilities are outdated and it is difficult to ensure the re-use of existing capabilities.	Keep enterprise information architecture maps current to facilitate the identification of capabilities that can help to fulfill new business needs.
IT executives are still lacking convenient tools to analyze the impact of priority changes in terms of resource assignment/allocation	Develop/acquire a tool that enables the automation of project prioritization as well as what-if scenario analysis
Securing funds is more difficult, even in the case of compelling project proposals.	Present a view of the project that emphasizes milestones that are relevant and pertinent to the business so that they can opt for a just-in-time funding approach.

4.2 Process Two: Managing financial and human resources

4.2.1 Purpose and key activities

This process drives the estimation and allocation of financial and human resources to various projects and other IT tasks. It requires forecasting future needs, developing a budget, designing a training plan and mobilizing the IT team (see Figure 4.3). The objective is to ensure that the company spends money and puts the best people on the tasks that best serve the business strategy. It is not just about getting the maximum bang for the buck. It is also about addressing any misalignments, assuming that business priorities drive IT priorities and IT priorities dictate resource allocation.

The process encompasses four activities, which typically involve various representatives from the IT, Finance and Human Resource departments.

- *Forecasting the need for resources*

  Generally, a member of the IT leadership team constantly assesses the workload for upcoming months to determine if additional financial or human resources are needed. Eventually, the forecast leads to new recruiting activities.

- *Budgeting*

  The next step is the development of the operating budget for current-year expenses as well as the capital budget representing future expenses. Over time, capital expenses are rolled into the operating budget as the expense year meets the current year. In addition, the IT team tracks actual expenses to uncover budget shortfalls (actual expenses greater than budgeted amounts). Eventually, the team requests additional funds from executive management to fill budget gaps.

- *Development of training plan*

  To ensure the successful execution of various IT projects, the IT team plans training activities. It produces a training curriculum that offers the opportunity to acquire the skills necessary to complete new tasks. Courses are delivered using e-learning solutions or traditional class settings.

- *Staff mobilization*

  Once assignments are established, the IT leadership team proceeds to set expectations for all staff members, including mentoring assignments. The effort concludes with the development of detailed performance evaluation documents.

Figure 4.3—Managing financial and human resources (process summary)

	Forecast resource needs	Prepare budget(s)	Develop training plan	Mobilize the staff
Input(s)	• Updated project encyclopedia • Utilization plan (current and future years)	• Resource management plan • Updated project encyclopedia	• Skills gap analysis	• Individual assignments • IT training program
Activities(s)	• Review skill sets in relation to assignments • Identify resource needs and skill gaps (over-utilization) • Develop new resource acquisition plan (profile, salary)	• Develop detailed operating and capital budgets • Identify budget shortfalls • Request additional funds (if necessary)	• Develop training curriculum • Schedule training events • Manage individual enrollments	• Establish mentoring relationships • Develop individual performance evaluation documents
Output(s)	• Resource management plan • Skills gap analysis	• IT budget (operating and capital)	• IT training plan	• Performance evaluation package

4.2.2 Concerns and proposed actions

Although the process seems logical and straightforward, it can be hampered by disagreements over funding and resource allocation decisions. If a manager does not see a benefit for its own area, he will tend to limit his/her financial contribution or oppose the involvement of individuals reporting to him/her. This situation characterizes large corporations with multiple business units. The process can be challenging and emotionally draining, especially when IT executives deal with a large project portfolio, have a limited staff and have to constantly request additional funds for critical projects that have been underestimated. The IT team should expect frustration as part of the process. The reality is that influential decision-makers will often tend to dictate the allocation of resources. It is critical to develop a good working relationship with influential players. Furthermore, it will be helpful to use "what-if" scenario analysis to help these players better appreciate the implications their decisions have in terms of team productivity and project benefit delivery. Table 4.2 presents a list of concerns and offers action(s) that can improve the execution of the process

4.2.3 Outsourcing issues and risks

To become or remain credible, IT executives must be able to develop realistic budgets, secure funds, provide exciting training opportunities, and effectively manage expectations for every staff member. Outsourcing such tasks would take away a unique opportunity to demonstrate a commitment to the success of each employee and a desire to seriously address their developmental needs. In addition, most tasks involve confidential and sensitive information.

Nonetheless, the IT team must consider the use of a convenient tool to expedite the process. It could eventually use external experts to assist with the development of competitive compensation schemes and exciting career development plans.

Table 4.2—Concerns/actions regarding the management of financial and human resources

Concern	Action(s)
Some IT mangers still use spreadsheets and lack a more convenient forecasting tool. They tend to overwork their staff, which makes it difficult to sustain high productivity levels.	Use a convenient forecasting tool to anticipate resource shortages and develop a tactical plan for hiring temporary resources to support the delivery of key projects
IT employees are often frustrated that their project assignments do not fit with their skills or development needs.	Be more flexible with the project staffing process by allowing employees to volunteer for specific project based on their skills and their development needs.
The poor estimation of project cost puts IT executives in a very uncomfortable position when they have to request additional funding for projects that are already underway.	Develop a tool to gather data, analyze project cost variance and gain the knowledge necessary to improve project cost estimation.
Often, recruiting activities are conducted through external staffing agencies that have earned the company's business because they agreed to a standard and often low billing/pay rate.	Be involved in the recruiting process and bypass these recruiting agencies if you wish to attract a good candidate and hold a chance of retaining him/her. Low billing rates often translate into a short tenure and additional recruiting costs.

4.3 Process Three: Executing IT initiatives

4.3.1 Purpose and key activities

This process focuses on the delivery of new IT capabilities. This critical process ultimately reflects the IT team's ability to deliver on its promises. The challenge is to deliver both the solution and the expected benefits (see Figure 4.4). Its most visible aspect is the planning and coordination of project activities that must be executed by a variety of professionals (e.g. project managers, business analysts, software developers and testers). The less visible one is the auditing of delivered benefits to evaluate benefit gaps and improve benefit estimations in the future.

To improve the delivery process, most IT organizations have established a Project Management Office (PMO) that oversees the planning, prioritization and execution of projects. Increasingly, they are using standard project management frameworks and methodologies developed by such organizations as the Project Management Institute.

The process includes three activities that require good process management, team management, critical thinking and communication skills.

- *Development of a Project Management Office (PMO)*

  This phase is about process management. The PMO includes individuals responsible for establishing and maintaining methodologies to improve project lifecycle management. PMO activities address team building and effectiveness, change and impact management (scope, risk, cost), problem solving, conflict resolution, quality assurance and progress monitoring. They also focus on the deployment of tools that automate reporting activities using a set of defined project management metrics.

- *Project delivery*

  This phase is about coordinating the execution of project activities, and ensuring the delivery of a quality solution on time within budget. Here, the team collaborates to resolve unpredicted technical issues and build a product that meets specified functional/business requirements. The team often interacts with end users and other stakeholders during test and review sessions to debate potential issues, gauge the level of satisfaction/dissatisfaction with deliverables and create a sense of shared ownership that leads to a wide acceptance of the final product.

- *Project auditing*

  Auditing is a critical activity that occurs at different points in time over the course of a project. It generally focuses on evaluating delivery performance and tracking of benefits.

Figure 4.4—Executing IT initiatives (process summary)

	Develop Project Management Office	Deliver project	Audit project execution
Input(s)	• Project documentation / encyclopedia	• Project plan and resources	• Audit schedule
Activities(s)	• Develop/maintain methodology • Develop quality assurance process and tools • Train IT staff • Capture lessons learned • Set/adjust priorities	• Develop/maintain project plan • Supervise delivery resources • Manage new client expectations • Resolve project issues	• Track delivered benefits and benefit variance • Capture lessons learned • Develop progress reports • Audit project quality
Output(s)	• Project management office	• IT capabilities	• Audit reports

4.3.2 Concerns and proposed actions

This process is still inefficient in a large number of companies because of the widespread proliferation of unstructured documents and spreadsheets. IT teams could significant improve productivity by deploying convenient tools capable of automating routine analytical tasks. This would free up additional time that the IT staff could spend on pure delivery tasks. Table 4.3 provides a detailed overview of concerns and improvement ideas.

Too often, teams consider a project closed when the solution is deployed and the tests are satisfactory to the end users. In the future, the mindset and practices must evolve if the team is willing to regain the trust of executive management by being accountable for the benefits, some which could occur after the project is complete. They must also promote the re-use of exiting capabilities to address future business needs and constantly evaluate opportunities to turn internal capabilities into marketable products.

4.3.3 Outsourcing issues and risks

Most companies are looking to outsource this process. So far, the various attempts have produced mixed results. It is important to remember that major corporations around the world (particularly US companies) were already entertaining the outsourcing of application development activities in the early nineties. Data confidentiality and security as well as quality assurance constitute major obstacles to application development outsourcing. In fact, there is a backlash because external project resources are able to hack into systems or use confidential data in a way that is harmful to data owners. In some cases, companies have engaged local talent to revise and correct buggy source codes developed by offshore programmers. It is important to note that the lack of control over project delivery will make it difficult to gain a deep knowledge of IT capabilities and gain valuable project delivery intelligence. This could undermine the IT team's ability to devise compelling strategies and tactics in the future.

Table 4.3—Concerns/actions regarding the execution of IT initiatives

Concern	Action(s)
Some project managers still spend a lot of time on administrative project management activities.	Implement a project portfolio management to support the process including the adjustments required by business priority changes.
Project stakeholders still complain that the IT team focuses more on technical milestones and lack a business view of the delivery process	Adopt a project design process that is driven by the changes in the enterprise information architecture and therefore emphasizes business milestones
Often, projects do not include enough testing phases and end up requiring considerable post-maintenance.	Adopt rapid application development and JIT session to constantly involve the end user, intensively test the solution and maximize user acceptance.
It is often hard for business stakeholders to trust progress reports because they have a limited involvement in the review process	Be more transparent by involving business representatives in the audit process. By doing so, the IT team will quickly know if it is off the mark and can take corrective actions before it is too late and before its costs more to remedy potential problems

4.4 Process Four: Designing and evolving the IT infrastructure

4.4.1 Purpose and key activities

This process focuses on planning activities involved in the design and deployment of the IT infrastructure. IT architects execute planning activities similar to those an urban architect conducts when he/she develops a new construction code. IT architects develop blueprints to ensure that the addition or replacement a technical component does not threaten the integrity and reliability of the IT platform. Typically, they map and establish linkages between business processes, business data entities, business applications and hardware components. They also lead technical migration activities and manage the details of outsourcing deals (see Figure 4.5).

Planning activities produce operational guides and provide a detailed documentation of IT capabilities. This documentation represents an important input into the strategic planning process as decision-makers often struggle to determine the impact of proposed technology investments on the architecture or the opportunity to leverage existing capabilities.

- *Developing the enterprise information architecture*

   At this stage, the architects develop an encyclopedia of all business processes, applications, data entities and technical components. In addition, they use a variety of matrices to depict the functional coverage of each application. In the end, they identify which applications support specific business processes, the data they enable users to manage and the technical components that provide the processing power necessary to make these applications work. This important exercise also shows the business processes that lack adequate systems. Most importantly, it produces insightful maps that are useful to conduct IT security and risk management audits.

- *Planning architecture transformation*

  Upon analyzing the functional coverage of the whole set of applications used in the company, the team is able to determine whether the application portfolio is fragmented or integrated. Based on this analysis, it can plan an integration strategy in order to minimize application interfaces that are costly to maintain and are often the source of operational issues. This often leads to the transformation of the architecture through the reconfiguration or replacement of the modules that are not compatible with or easy to integrate with other applications. Eventually, the company chooses to deploy middleware solutions that enable a seamless exchange of data between applications. An important part of the activity focuses on devising a plan and a detailed policy for addressing security breaches. Ultimately, the challenge is to continuously migrating towards architecture models that offer a better protection against security attacks, enable a more integrated application portfolio and provide a reliable technical platform.

- *Managing the outsourcing process*

  Executive management expects the IT team to develop a due diligence process that will guide the selection of potential providers. They also expect the team to address complex issues relating to contract management (i.e. details of service level agreements, governance process, pricing models), control the execution of operational change requests and effectively monitor the performance of providers. The activity requires the use of surveys and audits to uncover improvement opportunities or eventually recommends the severance of a relationship when the outsourcing provider continuously fails to meet expected service levels or important contractual obligations.

Figure 4.5—Designing and evolving the IT infrastructure (process summary)

Develop enterprise information architecture	Plan architecture transformation	Manage operational outsourcing process
Input(s) • Business plan • Project portfolio	• Enterprise information architecture (including blueprint and standards) • Project portfolio	• Outsourcing strategy/plan
Activities(s) • Develop/maintain business architecture • Develop/maintain data architecture • Develop/maintain application architecture • Develop/maintain technical architecture • Develop architecture standards	• Assess functional and technical quality of hardware and software components • Audit IT security and risk • Develop migration strategy	• Evaluate outsourcing service providers • Outsource IT services (data center activities, etc.) • Develop change management process • Establish service level and evaluation procedures
Output(s) • Enterprise information architecture (including blueprint and standards)	• Architecture migration plan	• Outsourcing management process

4.4.2 Concerns and proposed actions

Typically, architecture reviews occur at the beginning of a new technology cycle. It also happens when the business/IT strategy suggests a growth in business transactions or the introduction of new products/services that are likely to require new architecture components. Often, important architecture maps become outdated while the team spends considerable energy and time enforcing less important technical standards.

4.4.3 Outsourcing issues and risks

Relying on external consultants/resources to design and evolve the IT infrastructure is not a new practice. During the old mainframe days, companies heavily depended on IBM to design and manage critical elements of the enterprise information architecture. Today, the constant innovation in this area (e.g. on-demand and grid computing) makes it difficult for the IT team to remain the best source of technical expertise.

The risk posed by outsourcing is the excessive dependence on external providers who could ultimate control or dictate the company's IT strategy. The question is whether the IT community should rely on a few major hardware, software and advisory firms for this critical activity. The concern is that a monopoly of providers would undermine every effort to promote creative ways to derive business value from old assets. Rather, they will tend to dictate the pace of innovation and promote constant infrastructure modernization, which might not always be in the interest of companies.

4.5 Process Five: Managing IT operations

4.5.1 Purpose and key activities

This process focuses on the day-to-day activities required to keep the IT infrastructure up and running. Such activities include planning and execution tasks that take place in a protected area called the data center. Typically, IT operations define five classes of activities (see Figure 4.6):

- Asset management: equipment or software provisioning, accounting, configuration, deployment, decommissioning and disposal;

- Production control/administration: security management, job scheduling and execution (data synchronization across multiple instances, backup and archiving)

- Business continuity planning and recovery focusing on the design and periodic test of disaster recovery procedures

- Monitoring and production control: capacity monitoring (disk, desktop, network, server) and alert management (health, 24x7 availability and performance)

- Change management: development of master configuration plans, upgrade of software or hardware components across multiple instances

   In this area, companies use administration tools to automate and monitor operational activities as well as analyze the performance of the technical components (i.e. servers and network components) in quasi real time.

   The process involves the planning and execution of operational tasks and procedures, which often consume a large percentage of the IT budget.

- *Planning operations*

   The planning phase is about organizing the execution of operational tasks in the data center. Typical tasks include capacity planning, security administration and the support of critical infrastructure components enabling voice, data and video communication.

- *Executing operational tasks*

  Operational activities include the assessment of processing capacity (capacity planning), the monitoring of the performance of networks and servers, the prevention of security breaches and the generation of secure data backup files. Another important activity is the specification, acquisition, deployment and eventual replacement of technical components. These activities often require a close collaboration with IT vendors.

- *Testing the business continuity plan*

  With the growing threat of cyber terrorism, companies are investing in security audit projects and are reviewing their contingency plans. This is an area of ongoing concern as unfriendly individuals are able to hack into corporate servers from any Internet connection point on the globe. Often, business continuity plans are supplemented with insurance policies that cover the cost of potential revenue and equipment losses.

Figure 4.6—Managing IT operations (process summary)

	Plan operations	Execute Operational tasks	Test business continuity plan
Input(s)	• Enterprise information architecture (technical architecture)	• Operational plan	• Enterprise information architecture • Operational plan
Activities(s)	• Schedule IT services and tasks • Develop operational controls/manual	• Manage infrastructure security • Perform database and network administration tasks • Manage storage devices • Execute change requests • Manage other IT assets	• Develop/review business continuity plan • Evaluate insurance policy requirements • Execute periodic test of business continuity plan
Output(s)	• Operational plan	• Operative technical infrastructure	• Test results

4.5.2 Concerns and proposed actions

IT operations represent the area that is most impacted by outsourcing because most tasks are often executed with the assistance of product vendors or resources with specialized skills. Two major trends are creating a situation that is conducive to outsourcing. First, technology components are increasingly cheaper and companies are opting for immediate replacement as opposed to repair. Second, the introduction of "self-healing" technology components could result in the elimination of some technical jobs in data center operations.

4.5.3 Outsourcing issues and risks

Outsourcing IT operations is common practice. In reality, IT vendors and specialized companies are valuable partners, especially when they can provide quality service and handle data center operations in a cost effective manner. Certainly, IT vendors have the capability to do so, given that they are designing hardware components and providing the software tools required to monitor them. They also are able to ease the pain involved in the frequent deployment of software patches needed to fix security holes and remedy virus damages. The challenge for executives is to understand their cost structure and negotiate operational agreements that reduce costs while guaranteeing improved service.

4.6 Process Six: Providing end user support

4.6.1 Purpose and key activities

This process is about providing technical assistance to internal end users. Typically, a dedicated team of specialists forms the Help Desk and assumes support roles. They collaborate with IT vendors to take care of various requests and deliver training activities that minimize call volumes. The goal is to provide the minimum knowledge required for an effective use of internal applications and therefore eliminate frustrating experiences (see Figure 4.7).

Recently, the use of specialized software has increased productivity in this area by enabling the remote diagnosis of problems and the implementation of self-service support functions. Nonetheless, a major change is about to happen with the introduction of "self-healing" technologies, which could reduce the need for dedicated internal support staff.

The Help Desk function covers three major activity groups that involved strategic planning, task execution and performance monitoring.

* *Developing the support strategy*

  It is important to ensure that support activities cover all components of the IT infrastructure to cope with any circumstance that result in business interruption or the corruption of a technical component. Using the different elements of the enterprise information architecture, the IT team can identify the vendors, evaluate the quality of their support services and establish a sourcing strategy. At the same time, the team formulates a service level agreement and deploys tools to effectively track calls/tickets and coordinate the intervention of support specialists.

* *Providing technical assistance*

  The help desk documents the problem statement and creates a work ticket. It investigates the problem and dispatches the ticket to appropriate specialists following a predefined protocol. It has the responsibility to constantly inform end users about the status of open tickets and detail ongoing actions. It delivers training to minimize the number of requests reflecting an improper use of internal applications. It conducts support interventions using a multi-layer structure (support levels) to organize and expedite interventions. Urgency, scope and complexity are important criteria used to determine the roles and responsibilities of each support level.

• *Measuring service quality*

Here, the focus is the analysis of service performance in relation to expectations as defined in the service level agreement. The analysis also covers the performance of external support providers (i.e. responsiveness and effectiveness) and feeds contract re-negotiations. This is an important task because business executives are increasingly scrutinizing the service backlog. In fact, Help Desk data is becoming a standard component of executive dashboards.

Figure 4.7—Providing end user support (process summary)

	Develop support strategy	Provide technical assistance	Measure service quality
Input(s)	• Enterprise information architecture	• End user requests	
Activities(s)	• Create support strategy (issue categorization and multi-level support structure, etc.) • Develop operational guidelines and policies • Establish service level agreement • Develop/acquire helpdesk tool	• Resolve calls (call logging, work dispatching, etc.) • Develop help desk knowledge base • Provide end user training • Manage vendor interactions	• Measure performance against service level agreement • Survey customers (satisfaction, complaints, etc.) • Develop help desk dashboard and management reports
Output(s)	• Help desk operational center		• Performance assessment report

4.6.2 Concerns and proposed actions

The main area of concern is the communication with end users. Often, they complain about the lack of information regarding the status of their requests. As they become more technology-savvy, they wish to add value by helping with problem diagnosis (i.e. re-producing a bug, developing the problem statement, reconciling problem statement with support knowledge base items). It could be useful to review the script used to manage the interaction with end users. Self-service and self-learning capabilities could reduce support costs and mitigate end user's frustration.

Furthermore, IT executives must avoid the late training of Help Desk specialists in the case of newly implemented solutions. They should start it during the implementation project to give them enough time to face the inevitable learning curve associated with new installations. It is important to address the risk posed by the change in ownership that occurs when the product delivery team hands a new system over to the help desk. Table 4.6 provides an overview of concerns and desirable improvement actions.

4.6.3 Outsourcing issues and risks

More often, the Help Desk function is outsourced although the first level of support is handled internally. The challenge remains the collaboration with external support providers to quickly resolve issues when they arise. Outsourcing is not a risky proposition because of past successful attempts. The introduction of "self-healing" technologies could accelerate the outsourcing trend. It could eliminate the need for an internal Help Desk by shifting the focus from problem management to testing (something that the end user could handle on his/her own).

Table 4.6—Concerns/actions regarding help desk activities

Concern	Action(s)
Training activities are often limited to a few subject matter experts and the support staff and end-users do not take advantage of training during the deployment phase.	Allow support technicians and end users to take advantage of training during the deployment phase, therefore reducing cost and minimizing frustration during production.
Often the same training activities occur during the deployment of the solution and after the solution is handed over to the help desk	Ensure that technical support specialists are involved during the training phase that supports the deployment of the solution
Technology-savvy end users remain frustrated by the time technicians take to resolve problems that are apparently easy to fix.	• Develop a call tracking system that end users can access to obtain information about the status of their requests • Refine communication scripts to provide better information to the end user

4.7 Process Seven: Establishing a governance process

4.7.1 Purpose and key activities

Governance is the subject of endless and emotional debates because it ultimately delineates the sphere of influence of business and IT executives. The objective is to define the roles and responsibilities of various parties involved in the execution of specific tasks, including decision-making. It requires mapping critical processes, defining procedures and assessing process compliance (see Figure 4.8). The issue of governance goes together with the challenge of designing an efficient organization. It ultimately affects the business-IT relationship because it defines the protocol of interaction for all stakeholders.

The definition and improvement of the IT governance model starts with the identification and mapping of IT management processes. The next step is the definition of procedures that clarify the roles and responsibilities assumed by involved stakeholders. Finally, the team assesses the level of compliance with established rules.

- *Mapping IT management processes*

  This initial task consists of mapping IT management processes. In so doing, the team identifies the steps, the decision points and the actors involved in each step or decision.

- *Establishing roles and responsibilities*

  The team defines specific roles (e.g. owner, advisor, doer) and uses these roles to characterize the involvement of each stakeholder in the various steps and decision points defining a process. In the end, the team is able to get an understanding of issues relating to level of involvement, accountability or concentration of power. These represent the areas of concern that trigger emotionally charged discussions amongst business and IT executives. In addition, the team creates a simple tool to communicate governance rules.

- *Assessing compliance and effectiveness*

  The ultimate measures of the effectiveness of the governance model are the level of compliance with established rules and the quality of decisions. To assess the governance model, the team regularly conducts audits and suggests actions (including the modification of established rules and procedures) to remedy undesired situations.

Figure 4.8—Establishing a governance process (process summary)

	Map IT management processes	Establish rules and procedures	Assess compliance and effectiveness
Input(s)	• IT processes (IT value chain)	• Flow charts of decision-oriented processes • Stakeholders list	• IT governance model
Activities(s)	• Identify critical IT management processes • Identify critical process steps and decision points • Identify stakeholders for each critical process step or decision point	• Identify roles (owner, advisor, etc.) • Develop role assignment within the context of each critical process step or decision point • Establish new rules and procedures	• Audit decision-making effectiveness • Revise rules and procedures • Communicate modifications
Output(s)	• Flow charts of decision-oriented processes • Stakeholders list	• IT governance model	• Revised governance model

4.7.2 Concerns and proposed actions

Establishing a governance process is as easy or difficult as the executive team allows it to be. Although the power play ultimately affects governance rules and procedures, it is important that the IT team to participate in the development of the governance model. In the end, it must be able to better appreciate the rational and emotional factors to get over its own frustrations. This is important to develop a frictionless business-IT relationship.

4.7.3 Outsourcing issues and risks

In most cases, executive management tends to dictate the governance rules. It is difficult to imagine how this process could be outsourced. Nonetheless, executives should continue to solicit the opinion of external consultants to uncover creative ways to run their organizations more efficiently.

In general, successful governance models reflect the company's culture and the management philosophy of the executive team. Their active participation in the definition of governance rules is therefore critical.

4.8 Process Eight: Assessing the performance of the IT function

4.8.1 Purpose and key activities

This process focuses on the definition of performance metrics, and the development of management dashboards (see Figure 4.9). Recently, companies have moved away from periodic benchmarking to deploy automated dashboards that allow continuous performance monitoring. In doing so, they prevent the proliferation of spreadsheets and eliminate the workload created by the creation, verification and submission of manual and electronic reports. In addition, automated reports can be tailored to the information needs of various audiences.

The process covers the identification of relevant metrics, the automation of reporting activities and the analysis of collected data. The team often forgets to periodically examine the relevance of dashboard metrics to limit reporting activities to the ones that provide the kind of insights that form the basis for a reliable source of intelligence.

- *Identifying dashboard components*

  At this stage, the team collects a list of metrics from current management and regulatory reports. It also uses the process mapping exercise to identify additional metrics that enable an objective analysis of performance. The objective is to develop comprehensive business-IT dashboards to replace old ones that are strictly limited to business metrics. The result is a decision-support system with sophisticated analytical capabilities.

- *Developing a reporting tool*

  Increasingly, IT teams are deploying portals to provide a central repository of management reports. Produced reports typically cover a variety of topics (e.g. user satisfaction, cost/benefit analysis, supplier relationship management, project delivery, service quality, operations, architecture management, risk management, strategic alignment). Dashboards also enable detailed analyses (i.e. trend, sensitivity, correlation and other analyses). In the end, executive management is able to constantly discern negative trends, conduct root cause analyses and implement corrective measures. The idea is to enable continuous performance improvement.

- *Analyzing performance and IT business value*

  As executives face critical decisions, they often wish that had a way to determine where, how and to what extent technology investments improve business performance. This is a challenge that IT executives must also address if they look for the best opportunity to regain the total trust of executive management. In this area, success equates to the constant generation of new insights based on the application of various analytical techniques, including external benchmarking. For instance, one interesting field of investigation could be the study of correlated business and IT metrics. Through this work, the IT team will be able to identify the metrics that truly matter and build a more credible story to illustrate how IT improves the company's business performance.

Figure 4.9—Assessing the performance of the IT function (process summary)

	Identify dashboard components	Develop reporting tool	Analyze performance and IT business value
Input(s)	• Management and regulatory reports	• Dashboard structure	• Automated reports
Activities(s)	• Develop comprehensive set of IT metrics • Map identified metrics against critical IT processes	• Deploy the dashboard using a software solution (portal, etc.) • Set up report access management infrastructure	• Use external benchmarking to set performance improvement targets • Use internal benchmarking to monitor performance trend • Use correlation analysis to develop business-IT intelligence • Refine dashboard structure • Communicate results
Output(s)	• Dashboard structure	• Automated reports	• Business-IT intelligence

4.8.2 Concerns and proposed actions

Although most IT organizations have developed dashboards, they have not developed the type of actionable intelligence that could significantly improve the decision-making process. Another concern is the use of established frameworks (e.g. balanced scorecard) that overlook IT. As IT teams become internal consulting groups, they must learn to use proven process improvement techniques like Six Sigma to assist decision-makers in the IT management area.

4.8.3 Outsourcing issues and risks

The leadership team is likely to own this process despite the excessive focus on outsourcing. As IT teams implement new mechanisms to derive valuable insights from captured data and enable the creation of an internal source of credible intelligence, they will increase their control of this process. Outsourcing is likely to be inadequate, given that any good source of intelligence is always protected. In addition, the intelligence gathering process and the findings must be treated confidentially. There is always a risk that external, or even internal resources, could mislead executive management once they gain an intimate knowledge of the intelligence gathering process. The stakes are high and IT executives cannot allow themselves to fail in this area.

4.9 Case for action

The actions discussed throughout this chapter will undeniably alleviate the frustration of IT stakeholders. In addition, they will yield considerable benefits in the following areas:

- *Increased productivity*—The IT team could streamline tedious and time-consuming processes (e.g. budgeting) by eliminating unnecessary tasks, expediting execution and minimizing process iterations. Nonetheless, this re-engineering effort will not be complete until new management systems are put in place. These new tools should automate routine analytical tasks and the production of important reports currently generated using inefficient solutions (i.e. Microsoft Word documents or Excel spreadsheets).

- *Cost avoidance*—By gaining a deeper understanding of IT management processes, including important maps describing the enterprise information architecture, the IT team can avoid unnecessary investments in new solutions. This ultimately facilitates a conservative approach that results in cost avoidance and reflects a sensible behavior, given the new focus on "doing more with less".

- *ROI improvement*—The accurate documentation and analysis of existing capabilities will accelerate project execution because project team will no longer need to spend time on what is generally called AS-IS analysis. They could not focus on the "TO-BE" picture and quickly focus on defining the actions necessary to bridge any perceivable gap. Some of the proposed actions (e.g. the development of a reliable source of intelligence) will drastically improve project success rate and ROI in the long term.

- *Increased credibility and trust*—IT executives will be able to develop a source of intelligence that enables the intelligent management of IT. Most importantly, they will reduce the level of frustration with IT and empower executives to manage IT as a business. In doing so, they will quickly regain their trust and remain important advisors.

Nonetheless, IT executives must evolve to become change agents. They must foresee potential changes in outsourcing relationships and prepare to address potential conflicts of interest and disagreements. They must strive to establish clear roles and implement a mechanism for assessing the contribution of all parties to the successful execution of IT processes. No matter the sourcing strategy, the IT organization must invest in intelligence gathering to drive the revision of outsourcing relationships in due course and enable continuous performance improvement.

5

Institutionalizing performance measurement to develop credible intelligence

With the emphasis on "doing more with less", IT organizations feel the need to reduce costs wherever possible. Nonetheless, they are concerned that a strong focus of cost reduction might compromise the quality of service or the productivity of the IT team. The risk of failure is considerable. This new challenge calls for a more comprehensive analysis of important performance factors. Although, the measurement of performance is not a new concept in IT, it poses a variety of practical challenges.

5.1 An assessment of traditional performance improvement approaches

In the past, the pursuit of excellence drove companies to research and emulate "best practices". At times, they also considered using external benchmarks. Every couple of years, they would purchase benchmarking reports from advisory firms to gauge their performance against competitors or leaders in other industries. Quickly, benchmarking became a universal tool to bridge performance gaps with best-in-class companies. It drove business process re-engineering efforts but fell short of enabling the development of sustainable competitive advantage. By definition, it was only useful to poorly performing companies that desired to catch up with the best. In addition, common benchmarks did not always take into consideration the specific context and the peculiarities of each company. To make things worst, advisory firms requested the right to collect a company's data when it wished to take advantage of available benchmarks. This requirement will soon discourage many companies from using benchmarking services because they desired to keep their data confidential.

Although benchmarking was helpful to periodically reset performance goals, it was useless for companies performing at the level of best-in-class organizations. Companies realized that they needed a capability that would enable continuous performance improvement. The solution was the implementation of an internal performance measurement process that would support the creation of an internal source of intelligence.

5.2 Focusing on internal performance measurement and intelligence gathering

Disappointed in the traditional benchmarking approach and pressured to increase productivity, IT organizations have recently adopted a self-reinforcing improvement process. By emphasizing internal performance management, they hope to constantly make incremental improvements. In addition, they rely on contextual investigation methods (e.g. customer surveys, complaints) to make sure that improvement actions also address current needs. The idea is to develop a business intelligence capability focusing on IT. In other words, companies perceive the need to expand their business intelligence capability to cover IT. In so doing, they intend to turn collected data into actionable intelligence that will be shared, used and refined over time.

To accomplish this noble mission, the team must develop a more complete view of the scope of the problem. Too often, the debate revolves around the information management process and rarely touches on the issue of intelligence gathering. In particular, the information management process is limited to the transformation of data into knowledge and fails to include a feedback mechanism. In the case of intelligence management, the feedback mechanism exists as a way to validate and refine acquired intelligence over time. Figure 5.1 depicts the intelligence management cycle and establishes a relationship between data, information, knowledge and intelligence.

Figure 5.1—Intelligence management cycle

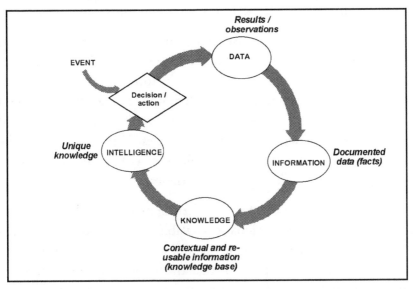

In practice, people collect *data* to understand the outcome of specific actions or decisions. This investigative task results in the documentation of facts supported by data and representing new pieces of *information*. Information becomes *knowledge* when it is framed in a specific context and becomes an instructive piece of information. As people share knowledge and test it in various situations, their success or failure reflects on the quality of acquired knowledge. Unique and validated knowledge becomes a piece of intelligence . For instance, any unique knowledge that enables the company to outsmart its competitors or drive the development of unique capabilities represents a source of *intelligence.*

Ultimately, the refinement and re-use of acquired intelligence improves the decision-making process. Individuals are able to make informed and educated decisions. Eventually, a source of intelligence could become outdated if it no longer applies to the business context. This eventuality justifies the continuous refinement of available intelligence.

A quick overview of a strategy-focused project can demonstrate the value of an intelligence capability. This example also highlights important aspects in the use of data, information, knowledge and intelligence.

Initially, a client raises an issue and commissions a team of consultants to make some investigations and offer a set of viable recommendations. The team convenes and starts a brainstorming session to develop a clear problem statement and a few hypotheses. They put together a work plan for gathering and analyzing any useful piece of *data* needed to validate or invalidate developed hypotheses. During this phase, the team uses analytical and creative thinking as well as industry knowledge to define a short list of good hypotheses.

Next, the team focuses on data gathering methods and presentation tools. Some team members lookup available diagnostic tools contained in the consulting knowledge base (i.e. questionnaires, analytical frameworks and templates) while others pick the brain of available colleagues who have a good knowledge of issues and solutions that could apply to the client industry or situation. The team executes data gathering tasks, analyzes collected data and reports the findings with supporting *information* (documented facts). At this point, the team reaches the proper conclusions as it identifies valid hypotheses that reveal the root cause(s) of the issues facing the client.

Later, the consulting team reviews root causes and use the *knowledge* developed during past projects to develop initial recommendations. They pre-present the recommendations to a few decision-makers to eventually garner additional *intelligence* and gauge the practicality and merit of potential recommendations. Often, a sound recommendation might not always work because of various constraints that represent barriers to implementation. The outcome is a set of viable recommendations with specific action steps and a detailed cost/benefit analysis (business case).

Finally, the team develops the final report with a story line for an oral presentation to the executive team. Sometimes, it chooses a member of the client organization and suggests that he/she delivers the presentation. In so doing, it establishes the type of close collaboration that minimizes communication issues and results in long-term relationships.

One key point is the importance of teamwork, brain power, communication and collaboration. The example of a consulting project demonstrates the benefits of an internal knowledge base as a tool that facilitates and accelerates the process. IT organizations must develop a similar capability, including a tool that enables the acquisition and instant update, refinement and validation of content. Traditional solutions do not always provide these features. The effectiveness of the process lies in the ability to structure the content so that it relates to specific elements defining a problem statement. It is important to correctly categorize the content in order to facilitate the retrieval of relevant knowledge/intelligence items from the knowledge base.

5.3 Developing and leveraging credible intelligence

To develop a good source of intelligence, IT executives must identify process decision points and develop specific insights that can improve the quality of decision-making. This effort should include process mapping activities as well as the test of various decision analysis techniques (i.e. probability analysis, hypothesis testing, regression and correlation analysis, value added analysis, trend analysis, what-if analysis, sensitivity analysis). The key success factor is the development of accurate and actionable intelligence. Ultimately, the viability of such a capability will depend on three factors:

- The reliability of intelligence sources

- The quality of developed intelligence

- The systematic and disciplined use of intelligence in decision-making

5.3.1 The reliability of intelligence sources

For a long time, companies have relied on advisory groups to get an independent and expert opinion on the benefit and challenges of most technology investments. They continue to do so and seem to embrace developed recommendations despite the potential bias towards suggestions that benefit those who fund them. The reality is that their backers often include dominant IT vendors.

Not long ago, companies took the advice of advisory groups and invested large sums of money into costly enterprise management and e-business solutions. They paid a hefty price for going with the flow and trusting the few success stories that dominated advisory reports.

In the future, IT executives should be more cautious and more inquisitive. They must demand that advisory firms offer a more complete view of the issues, including a discussion of failure stories and lessons learned. Otherwise, they will continue to expose themselves to costly mistakes. They must also welcome new ideas and value prospective vendors the same way they value their preferred vendors. These new vendors might well be the ones who have the desire to work harder to get the company's business. Because of their aggressiveness, they are likely to create the type of competition needed to fuel business and technology innovation.

Going forward, IT executives must consider other information sources such as direct client surveys to complement the picture presented in advisory reports. They must also consider developing their own source of intelligence through two activities:

- *Technology scan*

  IT teams must reinforce exploratory activities focusing on new technologies. By the way, these activities are less costly than remediation actions associated with failed projects. IT executives must remain mindful that openness to new concepts and increased receptiveness to new ideas are important success factors. It is the reason that they must encourage new vendors and find ways to get with a variety of organizations including academic institutions. They could consider joint research projects with these parties. In addition, the development of a large network of relationships will facilitate the validation of new ideas.

- *Knowledge base redesign*

  Often, decision-makers wish they had a reliable source of intelligence handy. In fact, companies have already implemented data warehousing solutions that enable data gathering and analysis. The challenge remains the ability to establish a clear linkage between the descriptive elements of a problem statement and the internal structure of any knowledge base. The lack of clear linkage justifies the redesign of existing knowledge management solutions. Ideally, end users should be able to query the knowledge base using criteria that mirror any standard elements defining a problem statement (e.g. business metric, issue type, functional area). Companies that do not have an internal knowledge base must invest in the development of this important capability.

  Upon identifying relevant internal and external sources of intelligence, organizations must make sure that the intelligence gathered is credible. It is equally important that intelligence items be easily accessible to decision-makers.

5.3.2 The quality of developed intelligence

The discussion about what defines good intelligence is an interesting subject for the reason that reliable sources can provide bad intelligence. Consequently, it is important to identify the attributes that define good intelligence. The logical way to address the underlying quality issue is to build on standard data and information quality attributes. In the case of intelligence, there appears to be ten criteria that relate to the content, form and time dimension. Figure 5.2 shows those dimensions and the criteria that apply to a source of intelligence.

Figure 5.2—The three dimensions of quality

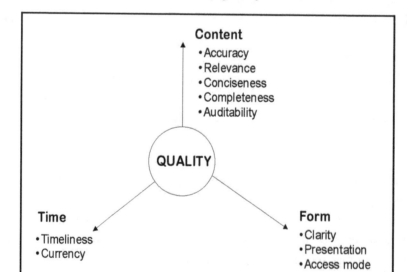

The *CONTENT* dimension is the most perceptible one. It defines the value of a piece of intelligence and focuses on its substance. Five attributes can be used to assess quality from a content perspective.

- *Accuracy*

  Intelligence acquired from reliable sources should be irrefutable and free of subjective analysis. It must derive from contextual, re-usable and corroborated information supported by facts.

- *Relevance*

  Intelligence must be relevant in the sense that it relates to a specific business or IT performance metric, be it quantifiable or not. This will enable the IT team to easily link problem statement and intelligence items.

- *Conciseness*

  Any intelligence item must be concise so that decision-makers feel confident that it does not require additional analysis to get to the real insight. Nonetheless, it must be detailed enough and supporting data should be accessible on demand.

- *Completeness*

  Supporting data and information must be complete and should include a description of analytical techniques (statistical analysis, surveys, etc.) used to reach established conclusions.

- *Auditability*

  The IT team must be able to trace updates so that users can identify the people who have taken the time to enrich or refine intelligence items. The goal is to facilitate the audit of gathered intelligence.

  The *TIME* dimension reflects the need to provide up-to-date intelligence whenever a decision maker needs it. It also emphasizes the need to keep the supporting data current.

- *Timeliness*

  Relevant intelligence must be readily available. It is important that the organization creates an environment that promote the systematic use of available intelligence by implementing alert mechanisms that automatically prompt decision maker to consider a specific item. It could even embed such mechanisms in operational systems.

- *Currency*

  The IT team must regularly revisit and continuously validate data that supports any intelligence item. An important task is the coordination and execution of a periodic review process. Eventually, intelligence that become common knowledge must not necessarily stay in the knowledge base.

  The *FORM* dimension addresses the presentation aspect. To design a convenient source of intelligence, the IT team must consider the following quality attributes:

- *Presentation*

  The IT team must evaluate a combination of narrative, numeric and graphical presentation modes. They must also take into consideration the preferences of decision makers regarding presentation styles.

- *Clarity*

  It is important that users quickly get to the point and that the information be presented in a familiar language. The IT team must institute a clarity test and use surveys to probe decision-makers about improvement opportunities.

- *Access mode*

  The system must allow the querying of the knowledge base and use such technologies as XML for content display. XML is a perfect solution to enable the collaborative capture, retrieval and refinement of intelligence.

The IT organization must own the intelligence gathering and sharing processes. They must consider a new role in the IT organization that will be responsible for it. *Intelligence czar* would be an appropriate title to describe this role. The key success factor is measuring process effectiveness using process improvement techniques and adequate metrics. Over time, the czar must become the internal expert in decision theory who oversees the application of decision analysis techniques across the enterprise. He/she must promote the systematic use of available intelligence wherever appropriate.

5.3.3 The systematic and disciplined use of intelligence

IT organizations must ensure that decision-makers always capitalize on available intelligence. As end users collaborate with the intelligence czar to develop and validate critical decision-making arguments, they will avoid the selective use of intelligence. They will eventually expedite the decision-making process because they will be able to quickly develop a consensus around important decisions.

Contrary to conventional thinking that suggests the secret handling of intelligence, companies must disseminate intelligence across the enterprise. One interesting exercise could be the review and evaluation of decision outcomes when decision-makers overlook available intelligence. Finally, the czar must proactively generate the type of intelligence that decision-makers value. Otherwise, he/she could become another technical subject matter expert who does not add value to the decision-making process.

6

Rethinking the practice of risk management

Recently, unstoppable security attacks have triggered a renewed interest in operational risk management. The lack of durable solutions almost makes IT managers nostalgic of the days when secure and reliable mainframe systems shielded IT infrastructures from hackers. Back in those days, business continuity plans consisted of building a secure and fireproof off-site facility to store back-up tapes and servers. If they wanted, they could purchase an insurance policy to cover the cost involved in redeploying an operational infrastructure. Life was easier because IT organizations could rely on one or two major suppliers to provide integrated technology solutions. Dominant vendors such as Industrial Business Machines (IBM) and Digital Equipment Corporation (DEC) evolved into one-stop shops. They could provide all components for a technical platform (i.e. hardware, software, network components, personal computers, mainframes, mid-range servers, sophisticated infrastructure management software and software development tools). In addition, companies could easily requisition on-site technicians to help with various tasks (security administration tasks, capacity planning, hardware upgrade activities) and ensure that downtime situations did not preclude essential transactions with customers.

Everything changed with the advent of the Internet. It drove the introduction of new e-technologies and the emergence of complex technical architectures enabling the distribution of processing power across a network of interconnected servers. As the Internet grew to become the backbone of new information superhighways, vendors revamped their solutions to make them Internet-compatible. New solutions would require sophisticated application servers and create a new challenge for IT system administrators.

In the beginning, the Internet was welcomed with enthusiasm because it promised to fuel business innovation through the emergence of online sales and distribution channels. It then grew into a universally adopted commerce platform connecting companies and customers on a global scale. Soon, it will create new security challenges that would hamper the growth of e-commerce. Companies could no longer easily encourage customers to transact electronically on their new web sites. Frequent denials of access by servers unfit to support high volumes of concurrent transactions deceived even the most enthusiastic customers. Unfortunately, some companies experienced revenue losses. The increased risk and complexity characterizing Internet-based infrastructures had become a serious issue. To solve the problem, companies boosted existing servers with additional processors or invested in robust machines. For instance, a few stock brokerage firms paid a hefty price for offering electronic trading services using unreliable technical platforms.

The situation worsened when hackers started spreading software viruses that could paralyze the IT infrastructure of companies for several hours or days. These viruses were able to defeat security lines (firewalls, operating system features) and completely shut down servers. Securing confidential transaction data became a top priority. The Internet had suddenly created a new breed of issues that highlighted the need to rethink the practice of risk management.

6.1 *An assessment of traditional risk management practices*

The lack of due diligence on the part of IT analysts who advocated the use of the Internet and promised a steady growth of global e-commerce proved to be costly for the entire business community. Security flaws were causing major frictions in board and executive rooms, adding to the disappointment with technology investments and fueling the frustration of IT stakeholders. The proposed solutions were firewalls and software patches but they would not eradicate the problem. The major concern was that major vendors did not have a clear strategy to solve the problem. They introduced new reward programs designed to encourage the denunciation of the perpetrators of virus attacks. If this initiative showed a commitment to address the issue, it fell short of satisfying the needs of businesses.

Companies were put on the defensive and resorted to IT security audit projects to attempt to mitigate operational risks. The goal of these projects was to identify the weak links along the data processing chain and develop audit trails that would facilitate the diagnosis and monitoring processes. Most initiatives involved a complete review of the enterprise information architecture and the investigation of every component (business processes, application portfolio, data models and technical architecture components). Unfortunately, this approach was only useful to assess the risk but not to shield the company from damaging attacks. They led to the development of operational practices focused on recovery procedures. It was necessary to develop effective risk management strategies and tactics.

As they thought about developing a long-term strategy, companies could not determine easy and viable ways to mitigate operational risks. They were entertaining the outsourcing of operational tasks to third parties who could track the large volume of new software patches that vendors developed and install them as soon as they became available.

Suddenly, outsourcing became an irresistible option. It also appeared that companies needed to improve risk assessment and rating practices to address risk issues at an early stage, given the fact that future technology projects would ultimately increase the current risk level. For the first time, IT executives did not object to releasing the control of critical tasks to third parties.

Although the use of outsourcing service providers became an appealing proposition, the true challenge was to create effective working relationships with these providers. At the end of day, the IT team would still be responsible for the IT function and they could not simply rejoice that risky tasks could now be forever assigned to external service providers. They had to prepare for the eventuality that unfortunate events might require taking back outsourced tasks. IT executives were also wondering how they could stop frustrated business peers from directly initiating negotiations with outsourcing vendors. They needed to figure out a way to collaborate with executive management, support such negotiations and promote smart outsourcing through the careful planning and prioritization of outsourcing opportunities. In addition, they thought they could contribute by establishing a process to continually assess the quality of established outsourcing relationships, including a review of sourcing options. Ultimately, business and IT executives could be able to put in place advantageous contractual agreements and cope with the challenges they might face if they had to sever a relationship or scale back an existing deal. Suddenly, IT executives realized that it was critical that they deepen the risk assessment process and get involved in the negotiation of outsourcing deals. Success in this area could help them to reclaim their role as trusted business advisors.

6.2 Emphasizing risk assessment and enabling smart outsourcing

Today, IT executives must implement risk assessment methodologies that have more depth. Common frameworks, including those developed by important research organizations (e.g. Project Management Institute), tend to confine risk assessment and evaluation to a quick walk through a predefined checklist. Such approaches apply best to a typical system implementation project. They would be unfit for analyzing issues that require open-mindedness as well as the use of creative, critical and analytical thinking to devise effective risk management tactics. IT executives must implement a risk management process that enables them to identify and better quantify unconventional risk factors. It is an important task, which cannot be the sole responsibility of a single project manager as it is the case with traditional IT projects. The process must leverage the experience and creativity of the entire team and include a thorough review and validation of initial findings developed by project managers.

In the immediate future, additional effort should focus on improving audit actions, encouraging the systematic development of risk mitigation strategies and implementing viable security measures. Beyond the immediate future, IT executives must shift the focus from auditing and remediation to prevention. Going forward, they ought to determine the intrinsic security risk of new projects and devise strategies to protect the integrity of delivered IT capabilities. It is therefore important to rethink the risk assessment and mitigation process to better address emerging and future challenges (security, mergers/acquisitions, etc.). Figure 6.1 depicts the kind of process IT executives must put in place to improve the risk management process. Improvements must be made at three levels:

- Risk definition

- Risk analysis

- Risk mitigation strategy development

Figure 6.1—Risk assessment and mitigation process

Risk identification	Risk analysis	Risk mitigation strategy development
Input(s) • Project documentation (charter, business case, etc.)	• List of qualified risk factors	• List of quantified risk factors
Activities(s) • Generate hypotheses • Identify risk areas/dimensions • Define risk factors	• Analyze risk factors • Measure risk factors	• Weight risk factors • Determine risk score • Develop viable risk mitigation strategies
Output(s) • List of qualified risk factors	• List of quantified risk factors	• Risk documentation

The process includes the identification, qualification, quantification and ranking of risk factors as well as the development of mitigation strategies. It stresses the use of a more analytical and thorough approach that contrasts with traditional practices. With the growing interest in outsourcing, it becomes important to consider all possible risk drivers, including underestimated notions such as speed-to-market or local business practices/culture. Such notions mattered less before the outsourcing era, but they will increasingly make the difference between success and failure. It is also important to note that the task is incomplete without the development of detailed risk mitigation strategies.

Risk definition

Generally, project managers are required to follow an established methodology that offers a predefined list of risk factors. By simply picking items from a checklist, project managers unconsciously or consciously assume that inaction will never be a viable option. This is one example to show that traditional methods do not always incite project managers to think creatively and critically. In the end, their assessment of risk is likely to present an incomplete picture, lacking one of the most poignant argumentation often used in thoughtful and compelling business cases. It is the fact that people are often more receptive to the risk of inaction than any argument for action. In a situation where stakeholders question the business case, a bias towards action might create the impression that the project manager is overselling the project. In the future, IT organizations should be mindful to consider the risk of inaction because it often is a more powerful argument. Risk definition must be a group exercise designed to generate risk hypotheses and validate identified risk factors using case studies, experience and logic. It is important that participants include IT and business representatives in order to start developing a consensus around proposed recommendations.

Risk analysis

Usually, project managers are able to qualify the risk factors but they find it difficult to quantify the risk. With the renewed emphasis on risk management, they must now make an effort to quantify the risk because it will become an important criterion for prioritizing projects. Ultimately, IT managers will be able to use such data to analyze the risk profile of the project portfolio.

Risk mitigation strategy development

Once all risk elements are qualified and quantified, the IT team must develop a strategy to mitigate any negative impact they might have. The team must consider an exit strategy when the project has a high probability of failure. Examples include projects that involve immature technologies or products that will not sell unless they meet a very short deadline. If by any misfortune, the risk is magnified to the point where a different course of action is warranted, upper management will be happy to know that the IT team is ready to enact a predefined contingency plan. A good example is a decision to roll back the flawed implementation of a complex enterprise solution.

In summary, the IT team must carefully assess the intrinsic risk of future IT projects. In doing so, they will improve the quality of decision-making, especially regarding outsourcing. To succeed in this effort, the team must develop a tool that supports the quantitative analysis of project risk. Rigorous risk assessment will also improve the estimation of project cost because project managers will be able to factor in the execution cost of risk mitigation actions. The qualification and scoring of project risk is an essential activity that must become a top priority for IT executives.

For decades, risk management has been the forte of financial institutions. The subsequent section analyzes basic practices (process), highlights the strategic drivers (strategy) and clarifies the context of the decision-making process as it relates to portfolio management. Lessons learned from the analysis of the investment process can be used to improve IT risk management and foster the development of viable project portfolios.

6.3 Examining practices in financial services

The purpose of this section is to highlight and learn from the practices at companies that are in the business of managing risk, namely financial institutions. The focus is the analysis of investment decisions using the example of a stock purchase by a portfolio manager. Figure 6.2 provides an overview of the typical process flow.

The starting point is the review of the performance of the portfolio against standard benchmarks (i.e. Standard & Poor 500 and Dow Jones Industrial Average). To generate an exceptional return, the portfolio manager decides to invest in the stocks of companies that recently exceeded the expectations of internal research analysts. He/she takes a closer look a selective list of stocks and proceeds to analyze several parameters (i.e. stock volatility, insider trading activity, stock split or buy-back plan). The goal is to identify an attractive stock that fits well with strategies set by executive management around limits, stock class or diversification. The portfolio manager runs a series of iterative tests to determine the stock that offers the best return for a minimal risk. He/she attempts to predict a potential loss of value over a defined time-frame using complex simulation methods. The challenge is to anticipate adverse situations that could require the implementation of a hedging strategy. If the stock represents a good investment, he/she might purchase it along with a "put" option. This type of stock option allows him/her to sell the stock at a predefined price at any appropriate time in the future.

The key observation is that the portfolio manager makes a decision at three levels. The first decision is the initial choice of a stock. The second decision is the determination of its impact on the long-term performance of the entire investment portfolio. The last one is the development of a risk mitigation strategy characterized by the purchase of a "put" option.

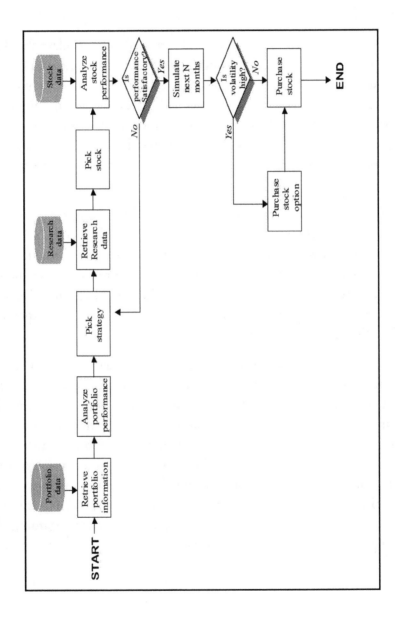

Figure 6.2—Risk assessment and investment decision in financial services

6.4 Applying financial services practices to IT management

To improve IT risk management, IT teams should emulate the decision-making process in investment portfolio management. They are already perfecting auditing procedures to address IT operational risk. Going forward, they must deepen risk assessment and mitigation practices to monitor their risk exposure and transfer risk to third parties when appropriate. This a key initiative that could be a source of competitive advantage in an environment increasingly affected by relentless outsourcing.

To improve the IT risk management process, it is important to keep a portfolio perspective. Generally, strategic fit and financial viability are factors that drive project prioritization. In the future, business risk and technology risk will become key variables in the prioritization equation as they become important management themes. They will drive such decisions as project freezing, cancellation or outsourcing and therefore affect financial and human resources allocation.

The proposed process (see Figure 6.3) emulates the practice at financial institutions. The objective is to establish an analytical process that ultimately supports the decision-making process regarding outsourcing. In an initial step, the project manager develops a compelling business case for a new project and computes the project risk score. Then he/she examines how addition of this new project will affect the risk profile of the project portfolio. Finally, the project manager makes a decision regarding the delivery of the project scenario. His ultimate sourcing decision is guided by available intelligence regarding the strengths and weaknesses of potential outsourcing service providers.

The key message is that outsourcing offers an option to minimize risk, given that the solution can be delivered with the assistance of external experts and in a cost effective manner. In fact, it is customary to use stringent contract clauses (penalty fees, strict terms and conditions) to produce the same type of stop-loss effect that a "put" option might have. In other words, outsourcing can be a good insurance policy if it is supported by a thorough due diligence process.

Unlike auditing, risk assessment and mitigation must be a continuous activity handled by the Project Management Office. There must be an emphasis on the active development of valuable intelligence in the risk management area. The impact of relentless security attacks justifies a renewed effort to better understand and address strategic and operational risks because IT vendors are not able to offer durable solutions. IT executives who adopt the proposed process or a similar approach will definitely regain credibility with executive management.

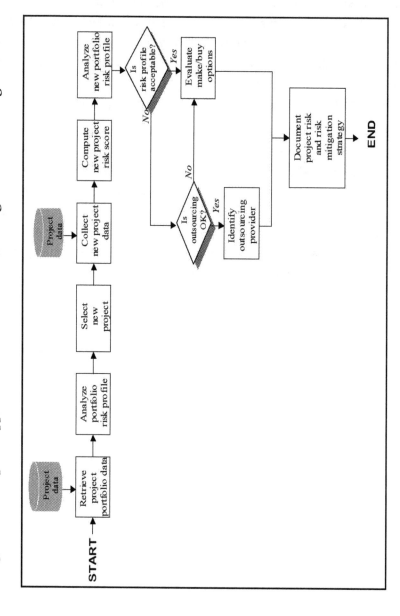

Figure 6.3—Proposed approach to risk assessment and mitigation in IT management

7

Crafting a new roadmap to business value creation

The future of IT can be debated but it is clear that technology is here to stay and companies should not see it as anything other that an important building block of the modern enterprise. It is therefore fair to say that technology will continue to matter. Nonetheless, what is unclear is its future role in the quest for competitive advantage and the creation of business value. This is a serious concern that calls for a thorough analysis of factors that will affect a company's ability to use IT as a strategic weapon.

As IT organizations focus on reducing cost, improving the security infrastructure and tweaking the complex enterprise solutions that run their operations, they will tend to favor actions that sustain the status quo. This predictable attitude could create extreme cautiousness and lead IT organizations to stop anticipating adverse situations that might reverse the positive results obtained so far. Already, IT departments are slowly experiencing a decline in productivity because the workforce is not able to bear the high levels of stress and anxiety created by the past recession and the growing interest in outsourcing. Such examples offer a preview of imminent challenges. As economic conditions improve and employees have more choices, companies are likely to face a crisis when overworked and undervalued employees decide to pursue new career opportunities with another employer in the same industry or a different one.

As companies continue to embrace outsourcing, they will struggle to manage relationships with dominant providers since they are already morphing into sophisticated consulting groups that could very well eat their lunch. In fact, a growing number of players in the outsourcing market are offering strategic IT services, gaining increased visibility in executive/board rooms and securing large contracts around the world. Consequently, IT organizations must develop a viable strategy to become or remain preferred business advisors. They must understand the forces that will shape the business-IT environment and ultimately affect the business-IT relationship.

7.1 The new environment

Several factors are likely to create new opportunities and threats for IT organizations. They originate from trends that affect the evolution of the internal and external environments of the enterprise. Unlike conventional forces represented in Porter's five-forces model (i.e. bargaining power of suppliers, threat of new entrants, bargaining power of customers, threat of substitute products or services, competitive rivalry), these new forces are rooted in the actions and changes of attitude by governments, employees and other influential groups representing the global citizenry. Each force (see Figure 7.1) has specific characteristics. All together, they create new opportunities and threats for the IT organization.

Figure 7.1—Future change drivers

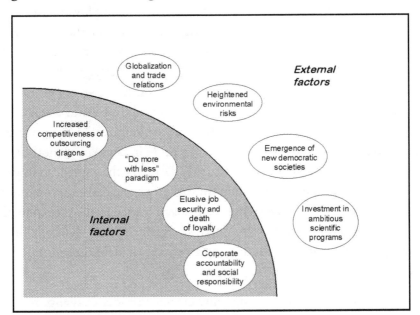

7.1.1 Internal challenges

Four factors create new internal challenges for business and IT executives. They require that the company leaders rethink their strategies.

The push for corporate accountability and social responsibility

Investor confidence has significantly declined with the recent revelation of financial shenanigans (i.e. misrepresentation of financial figures and frauds) at major corporations, which have also revealed ethical issues at accounting firms and investment banks. As a result, it is now more difficult to raise funds in the financial. In the United States, legislators recently introduced a new set of rules and regulations under the Sarbanes-Oxley law. This new law attempts to protect investors by making the CEOs and CFOs of public companies accountable for financial reports. So far, it has fallen short of reassuring investors because the compensation system continues to reward the executive who can boost stock price regardless of the tactics employed and their effect on the business environment, the work force or the long-term competitiveness of the company. In reality, as long as the benefits of fraudulent actions can exceed violation penalties, overly greedy individuals will always be tempted to violate the rules. More severe measures might be required to discourage excessive greed and instill a sense of social responsibility. This is important to reenergize the majority of small investors, who are looking to invest more in companies motivated by long-term sustainable value. Coca-Cola offers the perfect example of a favored stock since this stable company has decided to move away from the shortsighted management approach rooted in the provision of guidance regarding quarterly financial performance. Rather, they revamped their management team and decided to focus on running the business effectively.

The new push for more accountability creates a serious challenge for IT and business executives. They must prepare to invest in the right tools and implement the right audit procedures to guarantee the truthfulness of management and regulatory reports. This is a request that even privates companies must learn to fulfill if they desire to go public one day.

The increased competitiveness of outsourcing dragons

Countries around the world are seizing the opportunity to grab a piece of the outsourcing market. Governments in India, China, the Philippines, Eastern Europe and more recently Africa are transforming academic curriculums and implementing new programs to supply western companies with a pool of cheap talent. Today, the textile, manufacturing and information technology industries are deeply affected by the outsourcing phenomenon and this trend is likely to affect other sectors as soon as the needed talent can be supplied by outsourcing dragons. Even such industries as financial services are entertaining the outsourcing of research activities.

Building on their position as cheap providers of data entry, call center, and software development talent, outsourcing players are now going after more sophisticated and lucrative markets. They plan to offer off-the-shelf enterprise solutions and high-value business process outsourcing services. Recent job postings on the web sites of Indian outsourcing dragons reflect this trend. They are clearly attempting to capitalize on their cost-based advantage to dethrone dominant software providers around the world. It is not a stretch of the imagination to foresee a push to offer strategic management services, which is likely to create a tension in their relationships with internal IT groups. The scary fact is that these outsourcing dragons are rapidly adopting western standards and best practices.

The "do more with less" paradigm

Although companies adopted this paradigm to weather the tough economic conditions of the past years, upper management could continue to keep IT cost and productivity in check. Executive management is now used to actively analyzing surveys published by advisory firms and monitoring important benchmarks (e.g. IT cost as a percentage of revenue, IT cost per end user). As long as the information is available, they will put pressure on IT executives to continuously meet or exceed the performance of best-in-class companies. In fact, IT executives will be required to establish an internal audit process to track key metrics and determine ways to maintain productivity gains and cost savings. They must welcome this new challenge because they are in a better position than external advisors to set realistic expectations. Meanwhile, they ought to continue to use outsourcing to reduce risk and minimize cost variability.

The elusive job security and the death of loyalty

As outsourcing continues to create a sense of job insecurity in western nations, IT professionals will experience more anxiety and stress. Forced to reconsider career plans, they will attempt to join a more stable industry or take control of their destiny by following the path to entrepreneurship. This situation could dramatically change the employer-employee relationship.

For IT executives, the challenge will reside in their ability to maintain productivity levels with an increasing exhausted and anxious staff. They must prepare to lose even their most loyalty employees. Finally, they must find a way to keep a critical mass of valuable players.

In summary, IT executives must act on four fronts. They must strategize about ways to control the growing influence of outsourcing service providers. They must also institutionalize internal performance measurement programs to help executive management set realistic expectations. They certainly must provide solutions that enable the company to be in total compliance with Sarbanes-Oxley requirements. Finally, they must face the possibility of losing very skilled employees.

7.1.2 External opportunities

There are new external forces that will affect the competitiveness of companies in the near future. Unlike internal forces that will only bring new challenges, these will create a mix of opportunities and threats.

Globalization and trade relations

In the twenty-first century, large economic blocks have become the model for success. Undeniably, population size matters and it is not a coincidence if, so far, outsourcing has only benefited countries able to absorb a large volume of western goods and services. Highly educated and cheap professionals abound outside of India, China and Eastern Europe but these countries remain hot outsourcing destinations.

Although heated debates dominated trade negotiations lately, trade continue between western and developing nations. Additionally, the fact that India and China are attractive markets for western companies and that China is a major buyer of US treasury bonds has been a differentiating factor. In fact, western companies are supporting trade policies that open up maturing or attractive emerging markets. They dislike protectionism and argue that globalization is good for the economy. Certainly, it enables them to produce quality goods at a cheap price and ultimately increase their margins/profits in western countries.

In the future, countries that do not enjoy favorable trade agreements are likely to get together to form new economic unions. Upon uniting, they will organize and share the cost of investments in technologies that facilitate economic activities. Such initiatives are already changing the geopolitical environment (e.g. the New Partnership for African Development) since developing countries realize the enormous gains that the creation of a stable political and business climate could bring. By joining new economic unions, they will use their improved stature to initiate aggressive lobbying activities similar to the actions taken by Indian companies. There, IT companies have formed the powerful National Association of Software and Service Companies (NAAS-COM), which recently solicited the service of well-connected lobbyists to defend their interests in Washington. Even if they were not able to use the services of lobbyists, countries could demand that any new aid package combines credit lines and favorable trade agreements giving them access to western markets.

The emergence of new democratic nations

Undemocratic nations that possess abundant natural resources might experience a crisis in the future. They are likely to face a considerable challenge since the population under age thirty will become the largest segment of unemployed. Future leaders in these nations would have to open up wealth creation opportunities to their youth if they want to avoid explosive situations that could destabilize the country, especially given that it is increasingly difficult to migrate to developed nations.

It is likely that the world will soon witness the emergence of new democratic nations and the birth of an important middle class citizenry. As people aspire to live a life similar to that of a westerner, they will constitute a new customer base for western companies. As those emerging democracies join existing or create new economic unions, they will be able to afford new investments. Successful democracies will help their middle class prosper in order to generate tax revenues, assure the reimbursement of contracted loans and ultimate improve their credit rating.

Heightened environmental risks

As the world population grows and polluting resources damages the protective ozone layer, the community of nations is likely to re-enact and enforce treaties designed to limit the use of polluting and unhealthy substances. This is likely to encourage the development of renewable energy sources (e.g. wind- and water-based power generation systems) and the introduction of special combustibles designed to progressively replace automobile gas. Under this scenario, the world is ready to witness the transformation of many industries (e.g. chemical, energy, transportation). The future opportunities could require major technology investments and give IT executives another chance to be instrumental to the creation of business value.

Investment in ambitious scientific programs

Technology innovation continues to set industrialized nations apart from others and it is certain that those nations will continue to pursue ambitious programs to further their advance. Technology investments are likely to grow because they are synonymous with economic power. Moreover, they could result in enormous commercial gains in the future (e.g. spatial exploration projects sponsored by the NASA and other private groups). Eventually, such projects will lead to the discovery of new natural resources as well as the development of more advanced technologies. The gains could be considerable, especially in the medical, telecommunication, defense and transportation fields. Developed nations are also likely to fund and support new research programs at academic institutions.

In summary, companies that can develop a strong research and development capability (eventually in association with academic institutions) will be able to take advantage of new business opportunities created by new geopolitical, regulatory and social forces that are transforming the international scene. They must absolutely capitalize on such opportunities if they wish to grow.

7.2 Crafting the transformation agenda

IT executives have the opportunity to transform the IT organization so that it can create business value again. This time, they must make sure that they deliver quantifiable results. The first hurdle will be to resolve immediate internal challenges, which will require that they play a catalytic role and take specific measures to regain the trust of business managers. Nonetheless, needed changes should foster the collaboration with outsourcing service providers and emphasize internal/external relationship management. After addressing short-term challenges, they must develop a new vision to mobilize the IT team and capitalize on emerging external opportunities.

7.2.1 Short-term actions

Internal challenges represent the immediate obstacles IT executives must overcome before they earn the right to pursue external opportunities. The following agenda items define the short-term actions that IT executives must undertake.

- *Transform the IT organization into an internal consulting group*

  As companies institutionalize outsourcing, IT teams must operate with a consultant mindset if they want to remain or become trusted business advisors. In fact, the IT organization should do so to effectively collaborate with external providers, given that the most successful providers have leveraged the consulting model. Particularly, the IT team must develop new business management skills and figure out ways to derive business value from past and new IT investments. Going forward, the team must master the use of critical and strategic thinking, and the consulting model represents the right organizational approach. Eventually, IT executives would have to revise the compensation system and change the recruiting and training processes to motivate their staff as they tackle extraordinary challenges. In the case where the IT organization manage to be more effective than the best outsourcing service providers, companies should consider establishing an autonomous entity that is able to serve other external organizations and compete with outsourcing dragons. Established firms in the travel and financial services industries have already explored this evolution path successfully.

- *Perfect strategic and tactical IT processes*

Operational processes, which are major cost drivers in IT, are likely to remain the prime target of outsourcing in the future. The undeniable fact is that offshore outsourcing service providers have a cost-based advantage (i.e. cheap talent) that is hard to match. Consequently, IT organization must develop a competitive advantage around strategic and tactical activities. This means that they must improve the effectiveness of these processes and implement an internal audit activity to reevaluate outsourcing decisions and explore new ways to create business value. IT teams must continually reassess and be ready to cancel outsourcing relationships, but they ought to establish a fair process for measuring the performance of outsourcing service providers. It is therefore important that they keep their doors open so that new providers have a chance to present their capabilities and service offerings. Finally, they must identify circumstances under which outsourcing does not benefit the company.

- *Develop IT-oriented intelligence to enable smart decisions*

It is crucial that IT executives establish a mechanism to develop and share IT insights with internal stakeholders. This is one of the key initiatives they must implement to regain the trust of executive management and other stakeholders. They must leverage proven process management techniques and methodologies like Six Sigma. They must also invest in the development of an information warehouse and convenient tools that enable data/information gathering and the automated reporting of important findings. The key challenge will be to link the findings to specific performance indicators or decision outcomes. This foundational task will yield significant gains since it will empower decision-makers with a reliable source of intelligence. One area of benefit will be the automation of reporting activities that consume a considerable amount of employees' time. In the end, the IT team will directly contribute to the various activities that support the creation of business value (e.g. strategic planning, budgeting, project management, outsourcing management and auditing).

- *Deepen the risk assessment and management practices*

IT executives must rethink their risk management practices and emulate investment banks. To improve their project success rate, they must rationalization their project portfolio and develop methods and techniques to analyze the portfolio risk profile. Furthermore, they must find ways to re-engineer the project design process so that it supports a just-in-time funding approach. As they improve their risk assessment process and formulate risk mitigation strategies, IT teams will discover that outsourcing is a viable risk mitigation option. By designing sound practices, they will be able to enable smart outsourcing decisions. Success in this area will enable them to restore their credibility and secure project funds more easily in the future.

- *Implement effective IT audit procedures and tools*

IT executives can make an immediate impact by successfully enabling the timely production of accurate and verifiable management and regulatory reports. They must develop appropriate mechanisms (e.g. audit trails and data reconciliation processes) to remedy the misrepresentation of financial figures. They should also take the time to examine the strategies and tactics adopted by investments banks, where stringent regulations require the tracking of positions and limits in real-time, the reconciliation of front-office and back-office data, and the production of sophisticated management, regulatory and financial reports. Practically, IT teams can use the various documents describing their enterprise information architecture to examine the life cycle or critical data entities. This will allow them to anticipate data inaccuracy or data loss situations. By linking data entities to report fields, they could speed up the investigation of management and regulatory reports.

7.2.2 Long-term actions

Once internal challenges are resolved, the new consulting group should attempt to seize the opportunities created by globalization, trade agreements, geopolitical changes, heightened awareness of environment protection and increased investments in large scientific programs. In other words, IT leaders should formulate an agenda to capitalize on long-term opportunities. The goal is to create quantifiable business value in an environment shaped by relentless outsourcing. Suggested agenda items are as follows:

• *Continuously monitor trends to identify compelling opportunities*

To identify compelling opportunities, the IT team must collaborate with business managers and continuously screen emerging trends. While doing so, they must gauge their effect on the company's competitive position and identify the capabilities that are required to outsmart competitors. This discovery process must identify, document and prioritize emerging trends. In addition, IT teams must develop impact analyses and prescribe a viable course of action. Here, it is important that the IT team uses critical and strategic thinking to formulate compelling strategies. The output should be a list of product/service ideas and required capabilities that will feed the strategic planning process. For this activity, IT executives should set up a think tank structure to foster business-IT collaboration and idea/information exchange.

- *Develop a large portfolio of outsourcing and R&D relationships*

  The IT team must effectively manage and nurture relationships with external partners. The key to success will be an effective management of expectations and a clear definition of roles. These actions represented the minimum effort required to avoid potential frictions. IT teams must also anticipate the moves of outsourcing service providers and prepare to regain control of outsourced activities if needed. In the area of outsourcing, today's valuable partners could be tomorrow's competitors. It is the reason that IT executives must remain receptive to proposals from all potential providers.

  External relationships could also cover R&D activities. In this area, the IT team should try to take advantage of and encourage the funding of research activities at reputable domestic and international academic institutions. By establishing close partnerships, they could be able to use cheap resources to conduct feasibility studies, given that academia provides an excellent environment to corroborate analysis findings and test new ideas.

- *Focus on service excellence and revenue generation*

  To reach its highest potential, the IT organization must become a service/investment center. It must continue to implement cost-effective measures that are required to "do more with less" while maintaining or improving its performance in two critical areas: service and business value creation. IT executives must develop a strategy to empower IT employees so that they can pursue these goals with an entrepreneurial mindset. Re-structuring the compensation system will be an important action. Adopting a consulting model will be even more critical.

  By researching market trends and identifying opportunities/threats, developing a rich network of R&D/outsourcing relationships and repositioning IT as an engine of business innovation and growth, IT organizations will definitely regain the trust of executive management.

To successfully executive this plan, they must consider a strategic framework that takes into consideration the realities of the new era.

7.3 Strategic framework for the future

As IT organizations prepare to take advantage of new opportunities, they must avoid the pitfalls that lie on their path. They must recognize that although any major transformation program brings its own sets of challenges, good preparation leads to good execution. The proposed framework (see Figure 7.2) conceptualizes the issue of value creation for IT organizations in the future. It specifically highlights the need to reason like strategists and identifies important factors that will affect the value creation process.

Figure 7.2—New strategic framework

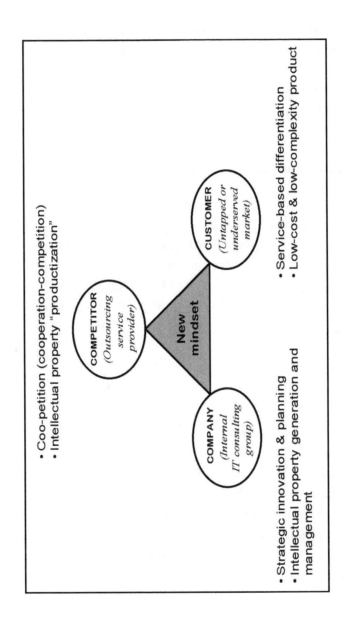

- Coo-petition (cooperation-competition)
- Intellectual property "productization"

COMPETITOR
(Outsourcing service provider)

New mindset

CUSTOMER
(Untapped or underserved market)

- Service-based differentiation
- Low-cost & low-complexity product

COMPANY
(Internal IT consulting group)

- Strategic innovation & planning
- Intellectual property generation and management

The framework assumes that globalization and outsourcing will remain dominant trends. It also draws on the analysis of internal challenges and external opportunities that guide the transformation of the IT organization. The subsequent sections discuss the three dimensions of the framework and highlight a few key success factors. This framework is unique in the sense that it goes beyond the traditional inward view that emphasizes the use of technology to improve business process execution.

7.3.1 Corporate dimension

The benefit of proposed short-term actions is that IT employees will develop the right mix of skills necessary to design compelling business-IT strategies. An appropriate investment in training and the redesign of the compensation system can instill the entrepreneurial mindset and sense of accountability that the IT workforce needs to succeed. In the future, the IT organization should capitalize on these capabilities to bring to bear a new breed of products. In this endeavor, they must find ways to leverage existing IT capabilities and analyze opportunities across industries and beyond traditional western markets. Practically, it means that the IT organization must encourage risk-taking and embrace any transformation plan that enables the organization to become a successful profit center.

In a global economy, IT teams must learn to collaborate with the marketing department to research opportunities in underserved and untapped markets. They must also address the challenges posed by currency exchange rates and intellectual property protection. They also must recognize that idea generation is an important process. IT organizations that do not evolve are likely to lose any edge to outsourcing service providers.

7.3.2 Competitor dimension

Initially, IT organizations and outsourcing service providers will attempt to develop a frictionless relationship but there is no guarantee that the situation will not evolve. Nothing can stop an aggressive provider from capturing the attention of business executives, securing larger deals and ultimately gaining control of the IT management process. Passive IT executives could become easy targets. This co-existence of *coo*peration and com*petition*, often called *coo-petition*, is likely to characterize most outsourcing relationships. To defend its advantageous position, the IT organization must watch the moves of outsourcing service providers as they attempt to be more than cheap software factories and call center resources. It should consider severing relationships when necessary. A well-designed legal agreement will not prevent a provider from turning into a competitor if the benefits of a new move exceed the potential penalty fees. Therefore, it is wise to develop several relationships, establish strict procedures to protect the company's intellectual property and measure the quality of relationships. One key activity should be assessing the strategy of a provider.

Outsourcing nations could soon witness an inflation of salaries that will undermine their cost-based advantage. In the end, we could witness the growth sub-contracting activities between dominant and emerging players in other developing nations. In other words, major players will secure large deals from western clients and outsource some of the work to emerging players.

In the case where the IT team and the outsourcing provider have complementary skills and enjoy their relationships, a revenue sharing deal could be the trick that forges stronger alliances. It is a good way to gain local support and thus manage to incite local governments to establish and enforce important legal frameworks that protect intellectual property and discourage computer hacking activities.

Anyway, IT organizations ought to take control of their destiny. It is too risky to remain passive.

7.3.3 Customer dimension

To seize emerging opportunities, companies must involve the IT team in the due diligence activities that are necessary to qualify the business opportunity, quantify the market opportunity, develop the proper marketing strategy and address other important issues.

To accurately quantify the market opportunity and develop a credible pricing model, the IT team can use the services of local consultants. They could also fund research programs at local academic institutions aimed at producing accurate market data on local emerging markets. In fact, they can solicit the services the local representations of the prestigious "Big 4" accounting/consulting firms. Proposed marketing strategies must have a global perspective and emphasizes a geographic diversification of the client base to minimize the effect of political risks.

More importantly, the IT team must consider a low-cost strategy to appeal to markets that are not ready to absorb costly or complex products. They must eventually customize products for various markets and incorporate self-administration and other critical troubleshooting features to facilitate customer support activities. Outsourcing service providers could help to produce at a low cost. It will be a prerequisite to quickly gain a dominant market share and win any price war that future competitors might initiate.

In the case of technology products, the differentiating factor will likely be quality of service, ease of use and the compatibility with local climatic conditions.

7.3.4 Promising perspectives

Future opportunities have the potential to offer significant economies of scope (i.e. one product could serve several industries) as well as economies of scale (i.e. one product could sell in various geographical spaces). These opportunities are within the reach of IT organizations that transform themselves into investment or profit centers.

In untapped and underserved markets, the IT team should be able to get the attention of potential buyers with a relatively small marketing budget, given that they are not as sophisticated as buyers in extremely competitive western markets.

After all, emerging markets are becoming the next frontier of economic growth. Although they are often victim of negative public relations campaigns, the potential for a relatively high return on investment justifies the relatively high risk. By the way, they are not more risky than western markets when it comes to affordable technology. The explosive growth of cellular services in developing countries provides an example of what happens when needed services are successfully repositioned in low-priority markets.

Many Fortune 1000 high-tech companies already derive a significant share of their revenue from non-domestic sales and continue to grow their operations in emerging markets. In fact, some companies are aggressively pursuing software deals in countries they never considered in the past. It is clear that new forces are changing traditional thinking and practices for the better.

7.4 Concluding remarks

The Relentless Pursuit of Information Technology Excellence summarizes the challenges often ignored by those who proclaim that technology no longer is a source of competitive advantage. It shows how the IT group can get back on the path to creating additional business value.

Undeniably, IT executives wish they could be empowered again to contribute to the bottom line. Those who have the support of executive management often lack a long-term plan. Figure 7.3 offers a point-of-view on the type of transformation that IT organizations must undergo. It is an effective plan because it addresses rational, emotional and political issues. This plan will help IT executives truly run IT as a business. It offers a very logical and realistic approach for achieving this goal, starting with specific actions to regain the trust of executive management and then generate additional business value.

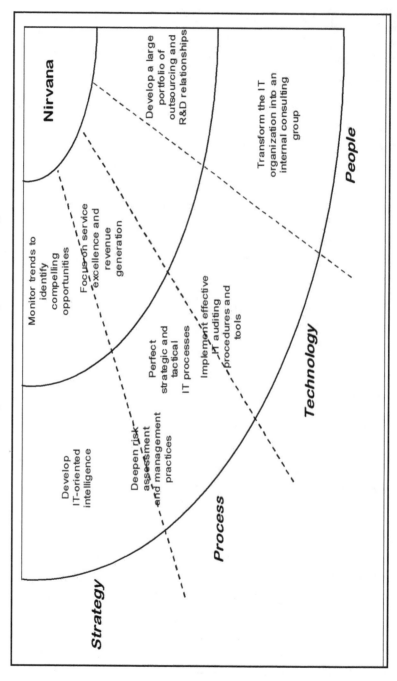

Figure 7.3—Transformation Map

The continuous challenge will be surviving the growing pressure of outsourcing service providers. Some companies have made the decision to spin off the IT organization and create a separate autonomous entity serving many clients. This could be a viable business model because it empowers the IT team and facilitates the migration from a cost/service center to an investment/profit center. Furthermore, it puts the IT organization on the same level as any external outsourcing provider and therefore eliminates important sources of challenge and frustration:

- Potential conflict of interest between IT teams and outsourcing service providers, which can lead to unhealthy relationship and poor collaboration

- Fair pricing of outsourcing deals

- Negotiation of short-term outsourcing deals (over a maximum duration of one technology cycle) to mitigate the risk to the company

- Pain and risk involved in selecting and nurturing relationships with stable providers in a market that is becoming highly competitive

- Resumption of internal operations if the IT team is put in a situation where it must regain control of outsourced services

- Potential charges (hefty penalty fees) when unpredictable situations require the severance of existing outsourcing relationships (e.g. merger/acquisition)

IT organizations must embrace change if they wish to survive. The ideas and prescriptions discussed in this book are important elements that they must integrate in their game plan.

Afterword

Not long ago, a friend of mine asked me what I am ready to do to help anyone implement the suggested actions. I responded that the content of this book reflects real-life challenges that I addressed or thought through in my professional life. In other words, I am ready to follow up on my suggestions and make them work for any interested party.

Recognizing that my effort would be incomplete if I could not stand ready to deliver results, I took the time to develop a set of relevant methodologies, training materials and software tools. I would therefore invite you to reach out so that we can discuss my suggestions, your challenges and any project that could benefit from my assistance.

Nothing would be more gratifying than knowing that my efforts contributed to one's success. I welcome your comments and inquiries. You can reach me at erictanefo@msn.com.

Bibliography

Peter Weill and Marianne Broadbent. "*Leveraging the New Infrastructure: How Market Leaders Capitalize on Information Technology*" Harvard Business School Press, Boston 1998

Neil Glass. "*Management Masterclass: A Practical Guide to the New Realities of Business*" Nicholas Breadley Publishing, London 1996

L. Paul Ouellette. "*How to Market the I/S Department Internally: Gaining the Recognition & Strategic Position You Merit*" American Management Association (AMACOM Division), New York1992

Michael Porter. "*Competitive Advantage: Creating and Sustaining Superior Performance*" The Free Press, New York 1985

Greg Brue. "*Six Sigma for Managers*" McGraw-Hill, New York 2002

Robert D. Austin. "*Measuring and Managing Performance in Organizations*" Dorsey House Publishing, New York 1996

Robert Austin and Lee Devin. "*Artful Making: What Managers Need to Know About How Artists Work*" Financial Times Prentice Hall, New Jersey 2003

Louis Fried. "*Managing Information Technology in Turbulent Times*" John Wiley & Sons, New York 1995

JamesA. O"Brien. "*Management Information Systems: A Managerial End User Perspective*" Irwin, Boston 1990

Kenichi Ohmae. "*The Mind of the Strategist*" McGraw-Hill, New York 1982

Ethan M. Rasiel. "*The McKinsey Way*" McGraw-Hill, New York 1998

Index

A

accountability, 21, 72, 107-108, 120

activity-based costing, 8, 29, 31

advisors, 0-1, 3, 5, 7, 9, 11, 13, 15, 17-19, 22, 26, 30, 37, 41, 79, 95, 106, 109, 113

advisory groups, 30, 45, 86

alignment, 3, 35-36, 50, 76

application servers, 13, 93

architecture, 7, 61-64, 68, 76, 79, 94, 116

AS-IS analysis, 79

Asset management, 65

assets, 3, 14, 30, 39, 49, 64

audit, 15, 23, 28, 49, 66, 89, 94, 96, 108-109, 114-115

automation, 8, 75, 115

B

backlog, 69

balanced scorecard, 77

bankruptcy protection, 14

benchmarking, 3, 11, 75-76, 81-82

benefits, 6, 8-11, 13, 15, 17-18, 29, 32, 34, 42, 48, 57-59, 79, 85, 108, 121

best practices, 0, 3, 11, 45, 81, 109

bias, 0, 51, 86, 98

blueprint, 0

brick-and-mortar, 12

budget, 0, 53, 58, 65, 123

budgeting process, 22

business case, 23, 85, 98, 102

business context, 49, 51, 84

business continuity plan, 66

business intelligence, 14-15, 82

business milestones, 35

business models, 12-13

business process, 0, 8-9, 29, 50, 82, 109, 120

Business Process Re-engineering, 8-9, 29, 82

business sponsors, 34

business strategy, 4, 24, 49, 53

business transaction, 9

business transformation, 0, 4, 7, 17-18

business-IT relationship, 0, 4, 6, 9, 11, 17-19, 25-27, 32, 72-73, 106

business-to-business, 12

business-to-consumer, 12

0-595-66712-0